# A MEANINGFUL LIFE

# A Meaningful Life

Graham Meltzer

Copyright © 2020 Graham Meltzer

Cover photo: By Mark Richards - Aurora Imaging
www.auroraimaging.eu

All rights reserved.

ISBN: 9798576934225

From my daughters.

To my daughters.

# Contents

Preface .................................................................. v

Introduction ........................................................... 1

Childhood ............................................................. 4

Values ................................................................. 35

Youth .................................................................. 46

Family ................................................................. 68

Midlife ................................................................ 100

Research ............................................................. 135

Home .................................................................. 164

Journeys ............................................................. 192

Q & A ................................................................. 242

Conclusion ........................................................... 279

Postscript ........................................................... 286

# Preface

This book of stories from my past is the end result of a Father's Day present from my daughters – a subscription to the website, StoryWorth, which facilitates the writing of memoirs. It arrived on June 20$^{th}$, 2020 as a most welcome surprise, not least because I was unaware it was Father's Day. Coincidentally, I had recently interviewed my 89-year-old mum, attempting to garner stories from her past that might otherwise remain untold. The principle of encouraging our elders to share their stories whilst they still can is a very worthy one, I believe. And whilst I do not anticipate popping off any time soon, it does seem appropriate to be writing a memoir at this point in time, threescore and ten years into my life.

The idea behind the book, as conceived by StoryWorth, is that the chapters be responses to random questions emailed to the protagonist once a week. However, not having a logical structure to the book stretches my credulity. So I have taken it upon myself to organise the book more conventionally, with a beginning, an end, and a sequence of linked chapters that hopefully form a coherent whole. Having said that, the questions from StoryWorth have definitely been valuable in setting themes and prompting memories. I have used them extensively, particularly, in the penultimate chapter.

I am aware that some of the book would be written quite differently by other participants in the stories it tells. So please take this portrayal of events as strictly my own. It is as accurate as my memory and emotional landscape will allow. Such is the nature of memoirs; they tell of the author's personal experience as viewed through a particular internalised lens, and that is all.

Writing this book has coincided with the 2020 Covid outbreak in the UK and around the world. The subsequent lockdown afforded sufficient time and respite from busy community life to enable me to pause, reflect, take stock, and document my life. The journey has taken me deeper into myself than I was expecting, which I hope comes through in the writing. I am extremely grateful to my daughters, Anna and Liberty, for their gift of the opportunity and the motivation to tell my life story.

# Introduction

My name is Graham Stuart Meltzer. I am the eldest son of Harry and Reva Meltzer (nee Jolson), father to Anna and Liberty Meltzer, and grandfather to Mattea and Kelson Keily (Anna's kids) and August and Miles Warden (Liberty's kids). My sons-in-law are Thomas Keily and Bradley Warden. To complete the family picture, my ex-wife and the mother of my children is Jane Meltzer (nee Evans). My siblings are Alan, Anne, John, and Nigel Meltzer. And I have a large extended family of numerous cousins, living mostly in New Zealand, Australia, and Israel. Our ancestry, going back three and more generations, is Jewish peasant stock, mostly from western Russia (now, Latvia and Belarus) with a splash of British on my maternal side. In the absence of a full dedication to this book, I wish to honour all of those mentioned above and put in writing just how much I treasure them, including those I have never met.

# Introduction

I grew up in New Zealand but subsequently lived for four years in between Israel and the UK, followed by 30 years in Australia. For the last 15 years, I have lived in Scotland. To the extent that I identify at all with any of these nation-states, I do so as a Kiwi. That said, I have become very attached to my latterly adopted home, which in many ways is not unlike the country of my birth.-

Me and my adopted home, Scotland, in 2014.

My life naturally falls into distinct periods marked by significant life stages and memorable milestones, which mostly determine the content and sequencing of the chapters to follow. *Childhood* covers the years from my birth to the end of high school, which coincided with my 18$^{th}$ birthday. The following chapter, *Values*, explores some of the thinking I was doing during my early and mid-teens, during which I developed values and principles that I decided to live my life by. That commitment I made as a teenager helps explain my choices, attitudes, and behaviours during the

## Introduction

following period, which I think of as my well-spent, misspent *Youth*, subject of the next chapter. It covers three years I spent as a student and the following five, up to the age of 26 when I met my wife-to-be, Jane, and a new phase began. The next chapter, *Family*, covers 22 precious years of nuclear family life, which ended with another unplanned divergence from the trajectory I was on. The chapter I have called, *Midlife*, covers the subsequent 20 years up to the present day, including the last 15 spent living in the Findhorn community in North Scotland.

Then come four stand-alone chapters. *Research* describes my investigation and advocacy of cohousing and sustainable community. The chapter, *Home*, describes some of the dwellings I have designed and/or built and/or occupied, and offers my thoughts on the deeper meaning of 'home.' *Journeys*, tells of travels I have taken throughout my life, but particularly since moving to Europe. The penultimate chapter, titled *Q & A*, provides answers to selected questions from StoryWorth that help fill gaps remaining in the narrative. And I complete with some concluding thoughts and a postscript.

I do hope you enjoy.

# Childhood

I was fortunate to arrive on this Earth into the arms of a loving young couple in safe and comfortable surroundings. I was born in Auckland, New Zealand, on December 1$^{st}$, 1950 (which happily, coincided with their first wedding anniversary). My dad, Harry (Henry) had fought in North Africa, Palestine, and Italy during WWII, returning to NZ in 1946. At the time of my birth, he was establishing himself in the 'rag trade' as a travelling salesman for the clothing manufacturing company, E. L. Riley. My mum, Reva, who was only 19, had been working as a nurse. Sadly, her aspirations of becoming a doctor had been thwarted by a father who believed that Medicine was no profession for a woman. She would have made a great doctor!

My folks brought me home from hospital to a small, rented flat in the Auckland CBD, but within a few months, we had moved

## Childhood

out to the suburbs. Subsequently, we moved several more times as the family grew and became more prosperous. It was the 1950s era of economic growth and security for all, particularity in NZ where a progressive welfare state provided universal healthcare and free education (including tertiary). Eventually (in 1959), my folks built an award-winning house in St Helier's Bay, a leafy beach-side suburb. This gorgeous home was where we lived for the rest of my childhood – my last few years of primary and all of my secondary schooling. Life was pretty damned good! But also, I was dealing with the challenges of being a shy adolescent working out who he was and what he wanted to become.

My folks moved from Auckland to Sydney toward the end of 1969. Dad had long since risen to management level at Riley's but ultimately left the firm to establish his own clothing manufacturing company, Harmel Pty. Ltd., a composite name derived from Harry Meltzer. The move to Sydney was prompted by a buyout of Harmel by JBL, an infamous NZ firm of corporate raiders that later collapsed with at least one of its directors going to jail. JBL had promised to establish and expand Harmel in Australia, but this never happened; they decided to dissolve the company, instead! Dad remained with JBL for two more years until its demise, then gravitated into commercial building development. True to his gregarious nature, he was very hands-on with builders, suppliers, and local Councils, enjoying the work for another 10 years before retiring early due to ill health.

# Childhood

The 1950s and '60s were a period of great prosperity and optimism in New Zealand (and throughout the Western world). Economies were booming, modernism had fully arrived, and consumption, particularly of fascinating, stylish, and affordable new devices, was endemic (unfortunately so, given what we now know about the environmental consequences of consumerism). On the flip side, the Cold War threatened nuclear annihilation, which so concerned my mum that she walked me in a stroller in Ban the Bomb marches during the early '50s. I do not remember the experience but wonder if it subconsciously primed the pacifist and anti-war protestor that I would later become.

My earliest clear memory makes for quite a dramatic story. It was the occasion when, as a three-year-old, I almost burned down our family home. We had recently moved to 4 McGowan St., Mt. Roskill, a typical suburban brick bungalow that, remarkably, seems not to have changed in 65 years. Below is a recent image from Google Earth, which shows the place almost exactly as I remember it. Even those miserable shrubs in the front seem not to have grown. The house behind had not been built back then; there were a garage and backyard at the end of the driveway instead. The photo shows the floor of the house raised off the ground. It had a suspended timber floor, underneath which was a crawl space that my parents used for long-term storage. There were packing crates under there, full of wrapping paper that had been used in the recent house move.

# Childhood

I have always been somewhat of a pyromaniac; well, who is not fascinated by fire? But as a three year old, perhaps I was a little young to be playing unsupervised with matches. I was home with mum who was pregnant at the time; she had gone for a nap with my baby brother, Alan. Seizing the opportunity, I took a box of matches down under the house and built a wee fire with paper and sticks. Having satisfied my curiosity and put out the fire (or so I thought) I went back upstairs to play with my toys and wait for mum to wake. I chose to play on the lounge room floor, which was fortuitous, to say the least, because sometime later I noticed the carpet feeling a lot warmer than it should. I put two and two together and ran out the back door and down the ramp to peer in under the house. What I saw will be etched forever on my mind – a wall of fire was consuming the whole of the undercroft, or so it seemed to my terrified three-year-old self. I had the presence of mind to run back upstairs and wake mum, who immediately called the fire brigade. I think they got there just in time to save the building. So the other abiding memory of the occasion was

## Childhood

the talking to I received from the fire officer. I can still recall being sat firmly on his knee and lectured rather sternly.

I was aged between three and seven when we lived in McGowan Street. The photo (above right) from the period shows my brother Alan and me, Dad with our dog, and Dad's mum, Vera (or Nana Vee, as we called her). This was the dog that suffered at Alan's hands, who several times threw it over the balcony railing causing my folks to pass it on to some other family. I have never been a dog person and wonder if that is due in part to this unhappy tale. Another deeply etched memory from the period was an accident that befell me when dad closed the car boot on my thumb. I remember the pain being excruciating and dad carrying me hurriedly up the front stairs and into the house for first aid. The injury resulted in a scar underneath the nail that I carried for decades. I think it finally faded about 50 years after the event. I remember too, a couple of go-karts that we had as kids; I think Dad made one and the other was store-bought. Our house was at the top of a mound, with the road falling away to a T-junction where, if you turned left, it fell away further and more steeply. We used to hare down the middle of the road at what seemed like breakneck speeds, seriously risking over-turning on the corner. Having just now viewed the streets on Google Earth, it seems that my child's brain may have exaggerated the gradient. But in any case, this was my first taste of the exhilaration of speed, a thrill that has never left me.

# Childhood

I spent my first three years of primary school in Mt Roskill, at May Road School about a kilometre from home. I think this must have been quite a confusing time for me, not least in respect of being Jewish in a predominantly Christian culture. Up to the age of five, almost all of my social contact had been with cousins and other Jewish kids. Once I started public school that changed, of course. I do not think I was made to feel different (although I would certainly know antisemitism at high school), but my imagination contrived some weird stories, nonetheless. Here is one example. Before walking to school in the morning, I would be reminded by my parents to stick to the *footpath*. But when leaving school in the afternoon to walk home, I would be reminded by my teacher to stay on the *pavement*. I had not heard this word used before to describe what I thought was called a footpath. So in my confused young mind, I imagined that Jews must use one word and Christians the other. I must have concocted this notion out of thin air due to a growing anxiety about being different. Another, less than honourable, memory of the period was my emerging kleptomania. I vaguely remember putting my hand up at assembly to claim lost money or property, whether or not it was mine. I have a feeling that this might have even prompted a visit to our home from a teacher or staff member of the school. It was not the last time I stole, I am sorry to say.

In 1958-9, my folks had a house designed for a site in St Helier's Bay, a leafy beach-side suburb in eastern Auckland. Whilst it was

## Childhood

under construction, we moved from Mt Roskill to Manurewa where our Aunt Freda, mum's beloved younger sister, had a vacant second house on her property. I recall this period a little more clearly and associate it with happier memories. The home in which we lived was another simple bungalow, but the property and semi-rural surrounds were more stimulating than the relatively sterile cheek-by-jowl suburbia we had left behind. Freda's double property had a swimming pool, tennis court, extensive gardens, and some native bushland. I recall learning to ride a bike on the tennis court and then, having gained some confidence, taken it on the road for the first time with limited understanding of left and right. I learned which side of the road I should be on the hard way. To this day, if I need a quick left-right reference, I recall the sight of a car barrelling up the road directly towards me. Having learned that lesson, I was allowed to cycle to school and spend time on weekends exploring the neighbourhood by bike. It was my first taste of freedom on wheels and I liked it.

Soon enough, the big day arrived when we were to move to our new home at 137A Long Drive, St Helier's Bay. I had visited the building whilst it was under construction, so the feeling I had on that first day was not so much of surprise, but relief – to finally be living in a house that was modern, exciting, and different! I do not mean to unduly criticise the homes we lived in before, but for someone with an architectural interest, even at the age of nine,

Childhood

our new home was a revelation compared with the stock standard bungalows of my prior experience. I loved its exciting spatial qualities, visual interest, and the way it was flooded with natural light. The image below, grabbed from the internet, shows the house (the one on the left), more or less unchanged, since we left, except for the addition of the pool and carport. I am guessing that the original double garage under the house has been enclosed.

Our house was situated down a long, shared driveway, so it was always quiet and private. The green strip between our driveway and the next was commons where we kids would often play. The two easements provided access to about six family houses (although there are many more now). I estimate that about ten kids lived in those houses, some of whom became friends. Below are two views from the street. The left-hand image shows our driveway and letterbox as I remember them. On that right are the letterboxes, nowadays, and tree-lined Long Drive running down to the beach, two kilometres away. Directly across the road is Dingle Dell, a vast area of natural bushland that became our secret playground and site of many adventures. St Helier's Bay was well serviced with primary school, sports ground, shops, cinema, and beach all within a walk. So in every way, coming to our new home was a bit like arriving in paradise.

The house had an exceptional interior layout spread over three levels with living downstairs and bedrooms above. The raked cathedral ceiling over the living area was about five metres high at its apex. Full-height windows allowed natural light to flood the space, whilst an adjacent sunken lounge felt more cave-like to me (the deliberate spatial contrast between the two being one of Frank Lloyd Wright's favourite devices). Best of all features was a bridge that passed through the space connecting the top of the stairs to the bedroom level. The left-hand photograph below shows the bridge as seen from the entrance and the other is taken from the bridge looking down over the living room. One of my most thrilling memories is of Alan and me jumping from there down onto the two large armchairs over two metres below, which was a forbidden activity, of course, but that did not stop us when we thought we could get away with it. Another banned activity that sticks in my memory is sprinting down the hallway and sliding in socks across the polished kitchen floor, which resulted

# Childhood

in at least two broken wrists, I recall. Is it no wonder that women live longer than men?!

The surrounding lawns and gardens were sloped and terraced which made racing around the house on our bikes all the more thrilling. The uppermost terrace (where there is now a pool in the aerial photo above) became a limited, but much-utilised, cricket pitch, whilst the double garage was available for table tennis and darts. Playing sport was one means by which Alan and I bonded throughout a childhood that also saw us at each other's throats on many occasions. I am still not sure why we fought so much, or so viciously on occasions; it must have been a nightmare for mum. Anne was a placid kid and younger, so immune from sibling rivalry (if that is what it was) in quite the same way. I am conscious of the futility of fighting with Alan to this day. I think on some level I must have felt especially guilty because I was the eldest child and should have known better.

# Childhood

As an aside, a Findhorn friend of mine has developed a theory about the personalities of eldest daughters – that they are more likely to develop a serious and responsible disposition. I believe that, actually, this applies to eldest siblings whether male or female and that for the rest of our lives, we can feel overly protective of others, which can spill over into being controlling. I know this certainly applies to me.

I attended St Helier's Bay Primary School between the ages of nine and twelve. The experience was mixed. I enjoyed learning in all areas except writing since I was, and still am, severely dyslexic. But I did manage to progress in everything else and bring home glowing reports. I enjoyed doing well for the intrinsic satisfaction it brought, but I also recall enjoying the parental approval it drew. I do not know why pats on the back were so important to me, as I am sure that mum and dad were always very encouraging. But I have often wondered whether my being so achievement driven as an adult is subconsciously motivated, at least in part, by a desire for recognition. (Or love, perhaps?) As one of four, and later five, siblings competing for attention, I think it is entirely possible.

I do not recall being particularly happy at primary school; I was shy and did not make friends easily. I related best through play – climbing on the jungle gym, playing marbles in the playground, or kicking a ball on the football pitch. My awareness of being

## Childhood

Jewish and therefore somehow different was exacerbated by the exemption I had from weekly bible lessons, during which I would sit in the playground feeling lonely and ostracised (although I was pretty sure that attending bible classes would have been worse and I was grateful for the exemption). For the first year, Alan and I walked the mile or so to and from school along Long Drive and St Helier's Bay Road. I think we were discouraged from taking the more circuitous, alternative route that passed through Dingle Dell. I particularly enjoyed the walk home because we had a shilling to spend on after-school snacks, which for me usually meant hot chips wrapped in newspaper, a 'food' to which I am addicted to this day. And I enjoyed having alone time to process. I recall that even when walking with Alan, we did not speak much.

I did eventually make one good school friend; I think his name was John and he lived right in the middle of Dingle Dell. By this time, I was riding a bike to school and permitted to return home with John along this once forbidden route, oftentimes stopping off at his home for a snack. His mother made us cheese boats filled with jam, which my health-conscious mum would never have done. If time allowed, he and I would explore and play in the bush; I recall a long rope swing being a favourite spot. Other lingering memories from this time include the quarter-pint bottles of free milk available at morning break, which were often left out in the sun and so quite unappealing. Much worse was the attention we received from the dental nurses on site. NZ in those days had free dental treatment for children and many schools had their own clinic. But they were generally staffed by interns and nurses, not qualified dentists. So the treatment tended to be clumsy and interventionist (a deadly combination). I imagine that a whole generation of kiwis, or perhaps two, have over-filled teeth as a result.

By now, I can imagine anyone reading this chapter might be feeling rather sorry for this poor lad. I do not want to give an impression of life being so hard. It was not, quite the opposite. But it does seem that the more challenging experiences feature more sharply in my memory. (I wonder if that is common.) So let me see if I can introduce some balance.

Our extended family life was rich in those days, which played out mostly on weekends with visits to our many relatives on both sides of the family. Nana Vee, dad's mum, had a home on the waterfront at Mission Bay that we would visit on most Sunday afternoons. Her deaf brother Harry, a truly sweet and kind old gentleman was often there too. These visits I remember well for the spreads that Vera put on. Predictable in their content and quality, they always included: salmon sandwiches, lamingtons, and pikelets with jam and cream. She was an excellent cook but that never stopped her from deriding her own ability, which I always suspected was to fish for compliments. But she was a

## Childhood

good old stick and passionate about sport, most of all cricket. She was a great supporter of dad's almost career in the game.

Our grandparents on mum's side, Pop and Nana Jolson, had a big old rambling house and garden that we loved to visit for the opportunities to play and explore. I recall climbing a prolifically fruiting red plum tree in the back garden and a moss-covered fountain in the front that felt like some ancient Roman relic. The basement was a favourite hang-out space for the traditional bellows organ and antique rocking horse, on which we loved to play. Pop Jolson was an intriguing character with what seemed like multiple business enterprises and hobbies including a farm on the Whangaparaoa Peninsula, north of Auckland. Nana J. was the sweetest little old lady you could ever hope to meet and the best cook. Her traditional Jewish cooking, particularly of bagels and matzo balls, was legendary.

The other folk of that generation whom we often visited were mum's Great Aunty Con and Uncle Bill. They lived in a classic Edwardian Cottage on the edge of Grafton Gully. In the days before a motorway carved through the area, it was a magical place for kids to explore. When indoors, we would play with packs of cards, building castles and towers with them. Aunty Con was also a great cook. I particularly recall her clove-infested stewed apple desserts served with custard. We also visited many of our numerous aunts, uncles, and cousins – way too many to mention here. And I fondly recall the annual Jewish Picnic held in beachside parkland, where we would have fun with the wider Jewish community. The Egg and Spoon, Three-Legged and Sack Races remain vivid in my memory. These were all happy, relaxed occasions that permeated a safe and stable early childhood.

We enjoyed wonderful holidays during this period. I distinctly recall several summer holidays in Rotorua where we stayed at the Ranolf Park Motel, shown in the historical photo above much as I remember it. Rotorua was a magical place for kids, with steam rising from the culverts along the street, the smell of sulphur in the air, bubbling mud pools and hot mineral baths. I remember those holidays with huge pleasure, as I do those spent at nearby Hamarana Springs with its crystal clear waters and fun boating activities. We also holidayed at beautiful Cowes Bay on Waiheke Island where I first gained a taste for fishing. And I recall once attending a dance in the small hall there when a '50s dance band was playing. I was mesmerised by the saxophone, an experience

## Childhood

which seeded in me a life-long love of the instrument. Later, in my early teens, our holidays were often spent with cousins at Red Beach, North of Auckland. We were very privileged as kids, to experience so many wonderful vacations.

I recall the beginnings of my interest in sport at this time. Dad would take us to Eden Park to see rugby matches involving the Auckland and All Black teams, and also to watch the cricket, his primary love. He was so keen to encourage us in sport, that he took on coaching the local soccer team for 9 to 11-year-olds, in which Alan and I both played. I remember feeling so proud that my dad was coach of the team.

I have one more story to tell from this period. I have only just decided to include it because I had an epiphany about the process of writing this memoir. I am enjoying it for sure, but then I usually enjoy creative writing (which begs a question about my dyslexia that I shall answer below). No, I think the enjoyment runs deeper than the usual pleasure I derive from written expression. It is actually feeling like a long-overdue confessional – a psychotherapeutic purging of guilt that has been forever rattling around in my subconscious. So this last sharing is of another event that generated guilt that I have always carried but never shared. I clearly remember the occasion when an Encyclopaedia Britannica salesman came to our home when I was aged nine or ten. He was very persuasive, of course. But the cost of the full set was prohibitive; I think it may have been about £500, which in the '50s would have been equivalent to many thousands, today. My parents were unsure about the expenditure; at least that is how I remember it. But the salesman kept plugging the lifelong benefits for the young lad sitting there (me). So when they finally did make the purchase, I took into my subconscious the responsibility for having caused them huge financial stress. Whether or not my memory is accurate, I think this is a good illustration of the kind of garbage that we all carry with us as adults that at some point needs to be acknowledged if we are to heal childhood wounds.

My childhood underwent a major transition in my 12$^{th}$ and 13$^{th}$ years, beginning with a serious illness at the age of 11 and ending with my Bar Mitzvah on turning 13 followed by the start of high school. It was a period during which a lot of childhood innocence fell away and I started to question assumptions about the stability and reliability of life as I knew it. I had known serious illness in the family before. Dad had suffered his first of three heart attacks at the age of 39 when I was ten. The event shocked us all, not just because of his age but also his presumed level of fitness as a keen sportsman. He was in hospital for a month and at home convalescing for weeks afterwards. Less than two years later, dad's brother Norman died of heart disease at the age of 42, a terrible thing that shook us all to the core.

# Childhood

In between these two shattering events, I experienced my own brush with death when aged 11. It began when I felt stomach pains sufficiently serious to warrant a visit to our GP who diagnosed appendicitis and immediately admitted me to hospital. I am hazy on exactly what happened next but understand that I was seen by students or interns who misdiagnosed the condition as indigestion and sent me home again. The next night my septic appendix burst, which caused a dangerously high temperature of 104 degrees and rampant delirium. I was rushed back into hospital where it took two operations to clean up the mess. I remember very little of those two or three days except for the delirium, which remains my most haunting childhood memory. It was a nightmare but without the visuals. I recall drifting excruciatingly slowly through time and space, with a level of consciousness but without much feeling or sensation other than a thick, soupy discomfort. I could not hear or see anything. But I felt an overriding fear of being trapped forever in this state of distress and sensory deprivation, drifting endlessly into eternity.

These three events: my father's illness, my own and Norman's death, coming as they did, one after another, profoundly affected my outlook on life. When I added in the fact that my dad's father, Joe, had died of heart disease at 66 (when I was four), I just assumed that the same condition afflicted all males in our family and so a similar fate would likely befall me. I became aware of my mortality much sooner than most kids of my age, certainly at that time. In an age before the Internet and social media or even much TV, children remained innocent for many years longer than they do now.

In my 13th year, I studied for my Bar Mitzvah, the symbolic Jewish coming of age as a man. This involved going once a week to the synagogue for a lesson with Rabbi Astor and in between, learning by heart the portion of the Torah that I would recite in front of the whole congregation on the closest Saturday to my 13th birthday. In those days, Bar Mitzvahs (and Bat Mitzvahs for girls) were a big thing, celebrated afterwards at a reception, which in my case involved hiring a venue and catering for 300 guests. I hated the fuss and attention being foisted on me and felt guilty about the expenditure on my behalf. The speech I was required to give at the reception was a total nightmare. For most of my life, I have had a deep fear of public speaking. Never was I more freaked out by having to give a speech.

Having survived that test of character, it was on to high school (Selwyn College) and my next major challenge. After working my way up to a level of seniority (and therefore self-confidence) at primary school, beginning again at the bottom felt daunting. All of my social insecurities came to the fore: shyness (particularly with girls, by this stage), having to make new friends, being different because I was Jewish, and so on. But on the plus side, was the opportunity for serious study. Because I had a bookish, academic bent, I relished the way that learning, particularly of the sciences, was taken seriously. I valued the teachers being specialists in their discipline and that classrooms were purpose-designed for each subject. I even enjoyed the additional homework.

My love of projects emerged at this time. In my first year at Selwyn College, I took on a self-directed project in Geography to study the USA by separately documenting each of the 50 States. I recall the aforementioned Encyclopaedia Britannica coming into its own during this time. I visited or wrote to dozens of embassies, tourism departments and trade organisations, gathering data, brochures, and publications. I can still remember the buzz I got from ferreting for more and more information. At the end of the project, I produced two thick volumes of findings, beautifully bound and presented. My love of research has been a life-long companion, ever since.

However, I struggled in some subjects. In our first year, we had to choose a language to study. I opted for French, which I soon regretted because the teacher was a bully and a sadist. I did not much engage with music lessons either, which is a shame because I would have a different attitude to the subject now. And I utterly hated bookkeeping. But, there were other subjects that I greatly enjoyed: mostly the sciences (maths, physics, biology (but not chemistry)) as well as art, woodwork and physical-education. My nemesis was English because my dyslexia made writing essays by hand very challenging. (There were no personal computers back then, of course.) I would endlessly misspell words by transposing letters and would usually have to rewrite the whole page when I did.

After mum read a draft of this chapter, she commented: "I never realised that your dreadful spelling was because of your eyes. I felt so, so guilty because it was caused by my contracting chickenpox when three months [pregnant] after visiting the hospital to see my nursing friends."

My limited vision has been a life-long companion and it warrants a mention. Mum tells me that my poor visual acuity was recognised very early, resulting in numerous visits to Dr Rich, an eye specialist. "We feared when you were just two months old that you would have little sight," she wrote. The condition I have is *Nystagmus* – poor muscular control of the eyes resulting in involuntary oscillation, which causes blurred vision. And I am short-sighted, as well. Nystagmus is only partially corrected by spectacles, so even with the best possible glasses, I never have 20:20 vision.

Dr Rich's prognosis when I was about two years old was that my poor sight would not stop me leading a normal life. He predicted, Reva says, that I would be attracted to the activities that were not affected by my sight and avoid the ones that were. Well perhaps

# Childhood

I can now be the best judge of that, and I would say that he was wrong. Poor vision has certainly been a disadvantage, but I do not believe it ever stopped me doing whatever I chose. And I am not convinced that it caused my travails with written expression. Yes, I have dyslexia and also, poor spelling. But I do not think they are the same thing, or even necessarily linked. Nor am I convinced that either is caused by my poor vision. At school and university, I needed to sit in the front row to even have a chance of reading what was on the board. And I have always had trouble reading signage and recognising people at a distance. But never has my poor eyesight prevented me from attempting something new or appreciating visual beauty, whether it be in art or nature.

A further challenge in high school was the perceived importance of English aptitude (or lack of it, in my case). Our 'home' classes in Forms 1, 2, 3, 4 and 5 (ages 13 – 17) were streamed according to our English grade only. So I would end up in the C or D class when I had the intelligence to be placed in the As. This was mostly a blow to my pride but also meant that I probably did not progress as well as I might have otherwise. Furthermore, much of the assessment was based on written examinations. In a time-pressured exam situation, my hand-writing was probably at its worst. To compensate, I soon learned good exam technique, apportioning appropriate time to each question and so on. I also benefited from after-school tutoring that my folks organised.

# Childhood

During my first year at high school, my brother Nigel was born some five years after the next youngest sibling, John. This pleasant surprise heralded the arrival into our life of a woman who has been an abiding presence, ever since. Mum and dad hired a specialist maternity nanny known as a Karitane nurse, which I believe is a role and a service that is unique to NZ. Judy would come regularly to our home (perhaps several times a week) and muck in with whatever needed doing, including spending time with us older siblings. She also stayed with us when the folks went away. Dad would regularly travel for work and, following his heart attack, preferred that mum go with him. Judy became a second mother to us and has remained a dear family friend until today.

Above are two photographs from the period. I am guessing we kids were aged 13, 11, 8, 6 and 1 when mum had that portrait taken as a birthday present for dad. The right-hand photo was taken some five years later when Reva was in her late 30s and Harry, his late 40s.

# Childhood

I have many fond memories of our domestic life at that time. The whole family would sit together around an open fire on wintery Sunday evenings, enjoying cheese on toast or Welsh rarebit for dinner. Family meals, generally, were almost always a treat. Mum was an accomplished cook and rarely served an average meal. Even reheated left-overs were presented with style. And her desserts were to die for. We loved going to movies at the Tattler in downtown St Helier's Bay, usually on Saturday afternoons at 1.30 pm. There was almost always a cartoon, a newsreel, and a feature film, usually a Western. And I well remember the purchase of our first TV, shortly after television broadcasting began in NZ. It had a small black and white screen and the first transmissions only ran from 7 pm to 9 pm, but still, it had tremendous novelty value.

My dad's passion for jazz was a huge influence on my nascent musical taste. We had a treasured radiogram on which he played 78s. His favourites became my favourites: Nat King Cole, Ella Fitzgerald, Louis Armstrong and so on. I still to this day listen to NKC more than any other vocalist. A further influence was dad's love of whisky, which he occasionally shared with me from about the age of 13. He drank Johnnie Walker Red, mostly, and JW Black on special occasions. I became increasingly keen on photography at around this age. Mum and dad were always supportive of my hobbies, not least when I suggested we convert our only storeroom into a darkroom. They agreed and also

# Childhood

financed the conversion. The room was perfect for the purpose and I spent many happy and productive hours in there over the next couple of years until one fateful night when bottles of ginger beer that I was fermenting on the top shelf exploded, one after the other, drowning the equipment and coating all the surfaces. So that was the end of that. However, photography has remained a life-long companion from which I have gained huge joy and satisfaction (and also a living for a short period).

From puberty, I was both fascinated and intimidated by girls. I did not date before I was 16, which in those days was not unusual; nor did I have a proper girlfriend, i.e., a sexual relationship, until I was 18, which was surely later than my male peers if their schoolyard boasting was to be believed. I foolishly took some ballroom dancing lessons when I was 13 in the hope that this might help, but they only served to cripple any interest I might have in couple dancing for decades to come.

I was fortunate to eventually fall in with a peer group of male friends with genuinely close relationships although, even amongst us, the teasing that went on could be hurtful. 'Good-natured ribbing,' as Kiwis and Aussies mostly see it, is endemic in the culture of masculinity in both countries. I was never able to compete at that game; I am just not quick-witted enough. But I am glad of that; I think it is a toxic cultural trait that causes considerable damage to many vulnerable boys and young men.

## Childhood

And whilst I am recalling painful experiences, the worst of these I suffered at the hands of a playground bully called Bradley who was big, burly, and extremely nasty. He would pick on me at every opportunity, mostly for being Jewish. This was my first real taste of antisemitism, although I do not think he was genuinely antisemitic (he would not have known, met, or read about Jews, at all). But my being Jewish worked for him as an excuse. Bradley and his gang would grab me and a Jewish friend and pin us against a wall whilst throwing tennis balls at us as hard as they could. Neither of us was capable of standing up to them and I was not inclined to snitch on them, which in retrospect, perhaps I should have done. So the bullying continued for quite some time until one day I lost my cool and aimed a vicious round-arm swing at his head. My fast-flying fist just grazed his jaw, which caused him to reel backwards and beat a hasty retreat. To my great relief, Bradley never came near us again, confirming what is often assumed of bullies – that underneath the swagger lurks a coward, or perhaps just an equally vulnerable kid who is abused at home. I gained a lot of confidence on that happy day!

My own gang of close friends (there were about six or eight or us) used to hang out after school, usually in the home of a guy with a full-sized snooker table in his basement. I soon gained a lasting taste for the game that was to draw me into some dodgy billiard halls when older. We also played a lot of cards – poker and 500 were our favourites. My enthusiasm for 500 turned out to be a precursor to my lifelong obsession with Bridge.

From about the age of 14, our gang developed an unhealthy interest in boozing. Our parents recognised the danger and successfully encouraged us to drink more responsibly by offering to put on a slab of beer for our collective enjoyment, but only within the confines of home. They much preferred that we drink at home rather than at parties or on a beach somewhere. So every Friday night we would gather at one or other of our homes for cards, beer, and camaraderie. I think this was probably the first time that I felt relaxed, comfortable, and sociable within a group of my peers. No doubt the alcohol was a factor in that.

In New Zealand at this time, you could obtain a driver's licence at 15, ridiculously young in retrospect, not least because there were no P plates. It was a full licence, which I gained easily following a few short lessons, an easy driving examination, and a simple multiple-choice test. Truth be known, I was driving unlicensed and unsupervised a year beforehand, but that is another story that I shall tell elsewhere. Having a licence and use of my mum's car certainly helped me gain popularity both with my mates and, more importantly, with the young ladies. Reva was always very generous with her Hillman Minx and a little too trusting since I was not sufficiently mature to be able to stay out of trouble. I had one serious accident a short time after gaining my licence and really pushed my luck on other occasions.

My elder cousin David and I had a mutual interest in fast cars and motor racing. We regularly attended the NZ Grand Prix (which was on the global circuit in those days) and races between souped-up production cars: Lotus Elans, Ford Mustangs, Mini Coopers, and other such classics. David had his own Mini Cooper with which we would tinker at length to coax the throatiest possible sound from the exhaust. On one occasion, I applied black racing stripes down the middle of mum's pale blue Hillman, which I recall generated quite some surprise when she arrived home that afternoon. Slightly less harmless was the drag racing from traffic lights in Queen Street that we enjoyed on Saturday nights. So much fun! And whilst I am in confessional mode, Alan and I were very keen on golf at this time. We would take mum's car very early on a Sunday morning to Remuera Golf Course, about five miles away. What I have never shared before was my attempt each week to beat our record for the quickest drive between home and the course. On one occasion, after overnight rain, I did a full 360 in the middle of Remuera Rd. I slowed down a little after that.

Sport was a feature of life in my early and mid-teens. I took up rowing and initiated a table-tennis club at school. But golf was preeminent; I deeply loved the game and have done so ever since.

# Childhood

It was one of Dad's favourite pastimes too, so it was an activity that Alan, I and he could share. There was a year or two when all three of us were members of The Grange, one of Auckland's top championship courses. I was also passionate about surfing. After I gained my licence, I was able to transport myself and a few mates to some of the best surf spots within a drive of Auckland. It was on such a trip to Waipu Cove that the abovementioned accident occurred. We had been planning the trip for weeks and were very excited. But on the night before we were due to leave, mum sat me down and said that she did not want us to go. She had had a premonition that we were going to have an accident. I knew mum to be uncannily accurate with her premonitions. She is a genuine psychic, a trait that I inherited to some extent. Indeed, she and I always had a very strong psychic connection, each of us knowing with certainty that an incoming phone call was from the other, for example. Despite knowing this, I argued that I could not possibly let down my mates and promised to drive super carefully and slowly. She relented and we went. True to my word, I drove as defensively as I possibly could. And yet we still had the accident. Nobody was injured (in the days before seatbelts) and the car was not sufficiently damaged to prevent us from completing the drive home. Nonetheless, it was pretty scary for all concerned and a valuable lesson coming when it did, soon after I gained my licence. I have not had a major accident since, which given my fondness for speed is gratifying.

## Childhood

As an aside, I believe that the two deep and enduring sporting loves of mine, golf and surfing, are related. They are the only two sports that I have enjoyed throughout my life, whilst plenty of others have come and gone. I think the reason is not much to do with the sports themselves, but rather the environment in which they take place. Both activities occur in 'natural' environments (although golf courses are clearly not fully natural). And both offer an immersive experience of nature in all its beauty (and power, in the case of surfing).

At about 16 and against my better judgement at the time, I joined the left-leaning Jewish youth group, Habonim. I cannot recall what drew me in, but it was certainly a life-changing decision. I had resisted for some years beforehand because Habo was fundamentally a Zionist organisation, focused on encouraging Jewish youth to settle on kibbutz in Israel. I had quite some resistance to Zionism, even as a teenager, however, I did have an embryonic interest in kibbutz. Through Habonim, I broadened my reading and deepened my understanding of progressive political theory. I have been a card-carrying socialist ever since and very grateful for the initial influence. And through Habo, I fell in with a whole new group of close and supportive friends. It was my first experience of deliberate and purposeful group (and community) building, which I deeply appreciated for the way it eased my shyness, not least with girls. I felt part of a 'tribe' and I was transformed by it.

# Childhood

Auckland Habo had a *moadon* (meeting house) in the city. We assembled there on Sunday afternoons for gatherings of our age group led by senior members of the organisation just one or two years older than ourselves. A range of activities was organised: educational, cultural, social, and recreational. We went on tramping trips and to summer camps. And for the first time in my life, I opened up to dance, learning traditional folk dancing in a troupe that would occasionally perform publicly. Writing about this now, it all sounds a bit naff but actually, it was perfect at the time, enabling me to find purpose and direction in life at a point when I needed it. The friendships I formed would accompany me through the next decade of youthful adventures. And I learned about the concept and experience of 'intentional community,' which would become a life-long preoccupation.

I am going to end this chapter here because the grounding and maturity that I gained through Habonim, effectively marked the end of my childhood and the beginning of my youth, if not my adulthood. In the following year, my last at high school, I became one of those senior Habonim members who took shared responsibility for a group of youngsters. And also, I met and fell for my first true love. This, I would say, more than anything, signified the end of childhood innocence.

# Values

I was "a mature child" my aunties would say, with "an old head on young shoulders." This is true, for at least two reasons. Being the eldest of a brood meant that I was often in a role, or felt that I was, of responsibility – looking after and taking care of my siblings. Being reliable and responsible (at least, in that role) became character traits from a very young age. Secondly, I was a thoughtful kid, blessed with above-average intelligence that I put to good use pondering the meaning of life, quite literally, and other philosophical questions: good and evil; right and wrong; the nature of God, and so on. Given my religious heritage, this is perhaps not surprising. But I went further with my inquiry. Whilst technically still a child in my early and mid-teens, I formed a set of values and principles, by which I decided to live the rest of my life. This is important to understand in respect of my youth proper i.e. late teens and early twenties, during which I was driven by a zeal stoked by them.

Our family was of the Orthodox Jewish lineage, which is neither ultra-religious nor liberal/reform; it is traditional and moderate – observing the Jewish holidays, attending synagogue and being true to the faith, but not rigidly so. We were not particularly *frum* (Yiddish for highly observant). But still, from as young as two or three, my siblings and I would participate in religious blessings, observances, and celebrations. We almost always, for example, observed the beginning of *Shabbat* (the Sabbath) before dinner on Friday nights. I remember these rituals fondly. They were short and sweet, involving the lighting of sacred candles, two or three prayers, a glass of wine and a *challah* (traditional Jewish plaited loaf). I recall a quite spiritual atmosphere of reverence and pause for reflection at the end of a busy week; they were precious and meaningful moments. And the meal that followed was usually mum's special fried fish, always delicious.

As a family, we would also attend the Shabbat service in the Synagogue on Saturday mornings – not every week but about once a month. I remember these somewhat less fondly; they seemed long, boring, and incomprehensible to me. The prayers and incantations were in Hebrew, which I did not understand. Even the translation provided in the prayer books was written in archaic English, or so it seemed to me at the time. The real value of these outings, as I saw it, was the opportunity to hang out in the front yard and climb trees with my cousins.

However, I do remember the building very well, with quite some reverence and awe. The architecture of the old Auckland Synagogue in Princess Street was striking, as is usually the case with traditional religious buildings. At the time, the earliest (colonial) public buildings in New Zealand were only about 100 years old; none were ancient and very few could even be called historic. The synagogue, therefore, held an important place in my early experience as someone who would later become an architect. It possessed qualities of spatial grandeur and visual richness that I do not recall being matched in many others.

From about the age of four, I attended Sunday School on most weekends. This, too, was not an experience that I much enjoyed. Sitting in a classroom reading bible stories that did not hold much meaning for me, when the sun was shining outside, was not my idea of childhood fun. It did not help that the headmaster was a strict disciplinarian who would apply a wooden ruler to the open palms of children he considered 'naughty.' So, looking back, I would say that my religious 'education' actually achieved the opposite of what was intended. Rather than mould me into an observant little boy, it probably birthed the rebel in me. Yet, the first values I internalised were in this religious lineage. And the first principles or codes of 'right behaviour' to which I was exposed were the Ten Commandments, which of course, feature prominently in Jewish religious texts.

Probably my most positive religious experiences of this period were the annual *Pesach* (Passover) gatherings, which in our family, were usually held at my grandparents' home. They were one of the few times in the year when grandparents, aunts, uncles, and first cousins would all gather in one place. They were grand occasions and amongst my fondest childhood memories. The *Seder* is a ritualised celebration where the story is told of the Jewish people escaping from slavery in Egypt some 3500 years ago. As the Old Testament would have it, this is when Moses received the Ten Commandments directly from God atop Mount Sinai. From the youngest possible age, children are encouraged to participate in the storytelling during the Seder, which is integrated into a sumptuous, ritualised meal. Indeed, there is a crucial role for even the youngest child in the room so long as she or he is old enough to sit at the dining table and engage. That role is to ask 'Why?' – 'Why is this night different from all other nights?' So this natural curiosity of the innocent child is something that is recognised and cherished in Jewish tradition. Indeed, I think it is fair to say that natural curiosity is a trait that is acknowledged and valued in Jewish scholarship as well. Debates amongst rabbis over the meaning of biblical texts are usually framed, much like the Socratic tradition, in terms of questions and answers.

## Values

I am not sure if this is what influenced me as a child or not. But I do know that I was intellectually curious from a very young age. Furthermore, I was suspicious of authority and very much a sceptic. I would question rules, regulations, and the status quo. I would critique mores and conventions that I think most kids took for granted. By the age of 10 or 12, for example, I had decided there was no such thing as God, and that the whole notion was simply a construct. I held this view for much the same (perhaps simplistic) reason that Bertrand Russell, Stephen Fry, and other atheists offer. Namely, that the Judeo-Christian notion of an omniscient, omnipotent, beneficent God makes no sense given the existence of so much chaos, pain, and strife in the world.

My cynicism deepened when, at about the age of 14, I discovered existentialist literature. I deeply loved Hermann Hesse's novels, reading some of them repeatedly. And similarly, I devoured the books of Camus and Kafka, although I found some of their narratives ominous and frightening, as I did Orwell's and Huxley's. Some of these books were required reading at school. But actually, they really spoke to me at a particular time in my life when my latent nihilism was bubbling to the surface.

Needless to say, I struggled as an angst-ridden early teenager, to make much sense of life, convinced that there was no God therefore no God-given guidance by which to live one's life. It threw into doubt even the Ten Commandments. Indeed, there did not even seem to be any ostensible, irrefutable meaning to life. And certainly, no heaven! I have never believed in an afterlife, as such. I studied science at school and university and in time became a social scientist. I value the scientific method to this day, taking nothing at face value and seeking evidence for any concept that stretches my credulity (such as the angels, devas and nature spirits that feature so strongly in Findhorn's history and culture). My scepticism, I am pleased to say, is now more muted, thanks to having lived in Findhorn for 15 years.

So what was I to do as a confused but curious teenager? I did what I do to this day when faced with any sort of deep question – I researched. I broadened my reading and sought meaning in philosophy, psychology, and the social sciences. And based on what I learned, I reasoned. I decided that if I am right and the gift of a human life is all that there is (i.e., there is no before- or afterlife), then I damned well better make the most of it, else waste a unique and precious opportunity. Based on my reading over several years, I gradually gained a humanist perspective. Key influences included: Joseph Campbell, Carl Jung, Erich Fromm, R. D. Laing, A. S. Neill and then later when studying philosophy at UNSW, Spinoza, Descartes, and Kant. I came to believe that we humans are born with enormous potential for growth, insight, development, and achievement. And yet sadly it seemed, most of us never realise more than, what? 10%? 5%? 1% of that potential? I began to see the fulfilling of human potential as that which gives meaning to life.

When I hit mid-teens (15 – 17 years of age) my reading and thinking broadened further. Major influences on me at this time came unexpectedly from Eastern spirituality which conveniently did not countenance a single omnipotent deity as in the Judeo-Christian tradition. The first such book to knock my socks off was Pramahansa Yogananda's Autobiography of a Yogi. It left a deep and abiding impression. And at about the same time, I was soaking up Kahlil Gibran. A bit later it was Krishnamurti. From about 17 or so, I read just about everything Krishnamurti had ever written (which was a lot!). And later still, would come Ram Dass, Alan Watts, and Thich Nhat Hanh. All of these wise souls spoke to me of human dignity, personal growth, and the power of love.

Some of my teachers

With their invaluable input, I ultimately came up with a home-spun ethos of my own that I believed I could live by and make sense of life. I reasoned that *creativity* is a key potential that remains unfulfilled in most people. Homo sapiens are innately creative (perhaps uniquely so) as evidenced by our extraordinary cultural development. Surely, creativity is one of our primary drivers as humans. And yet as individuals, most of us rarely fulfil, or even tap, our creative potential. So I resolved there and then, to strive as best I could in life to develop my creativity. However, I was wary of this becoming an individualistic, self-serving pursuit, which perhaps plays out most starkly in US culture. The NZ in which I grew up was in many ways the opposite; if anything, a 'tall poppy' syndrome prevailed. It was generally egalitarian, with little or no poverty and very few millionaires. And having also read the kind of left-wing political literature prevalent in the '60s, which was also promulgated in Habonim, I had developed a strongly socialist streak. Key influences there included Karl Marx, Peter Kropotkin and later, Murray Bookchin. So the notion of a self-absorbed drive to realise one's creative potential, if it were at cost to others, was anathema.

The value of *service* seemed to address the conundrum. This arises from the notion that we are embedded within society and deeply indebted to it, directly and indirectly, for our socialisation, education, wellbeing, etc. If developing one's creativity was about meeting the needs of the individual, then acts of service provided the opportunity to give something back. So it seemed equally important to realise one's potential in service – to family, community, society, and the planet. Happy with that, I still felt something was missing – something that tied these two impulses (creativity and service) together, integrating or unifying them somehow. *Love* provided the answer. I reasoned that whatever one does, should be done with love, and that the third imperative by which I would live my life would be to deepen into love in its various manifestations. I would pursue greater creativity with love and seek to serve with love. And I would love, with love.

So there you have it – my home-spun, tripartite raison d'être. I saw these three impulses – creativity, service, and love – as a kind of holy trinity. Developing my potential in these three areas would be my purpose, my code of conduct and my 'religion.' And so it has been my whole life. Whenever I have a decision to make, large or small, I measure it against these three criteria and decide accordingly. I ask, 'What choice will enable me to best cultivate creativity and/or service and/or love?' It is as easy and as difficult as that. I say difficult because I have not walked this path without tripping occasionally.

To conclude this short chapter on values and principles, let me try to summarise. To begin, I would argue that values and principles are different. 'Values' are qualities that one lives by that are mostly felt intuitively in the heart or gut. 'Principles,' on the other hand, are rules or codes of conduct that guide or direct our actions. They originate and play out in the mind. When I

# Values

Googled 'values versus principles' to check on this, I got: "Values are qualities that inform the behaviour of a person and principles are rules or beliefs that govern actions." So the internet confirmed my take, more or less. Values are qualities that we feel are important (like honesty, for example) and that guide our behaviour. Principles are more reasoned, and they help us make choices ('I will not steal,' for example). Interestingly, these two examples (honesty and stealing) are not mutually exclusive. I can imagine it is possible to value honesty and still steal in a given situation. In the movie *Shawshank Redemption*, for example, Andy Dufresne stole money from the cruel and corrupt prison master and I, for one, did not judge him to be dishonest.

Anyway, my values include, but are not limited to, the following:
1. creativity, service, and love;
2. authenticity, transparency, and kindness;
3. fairness, justice, and equality.

They are grouped this way because they apply to three different domains. The first group (creativity, service, and love) are my personal aspirations, as outlined above. They determine how I live my life as an individual. The second group (authenticity, transparency, and kindness) are the qualities that I value in social relationships and they apply mostly at the scale of community. In fact, they have become important to me exactly because of my communal living experience. The third three (fairness, justice, and equality) have an even wider, societal, and political, connotation. They are, I believe, how society should treat its members, especially the weak and powerless. A quote from Mahatma Gandhi comes to mind here: "The true measure of any society can be found in how it treats its most vulnerable members."

So finally then, what are my principles? Well actually, they flow directly from the listing of values above.

1. I seek to fulfil my potential in creativity, service, and love.

2. I strive to relate to others with authenticity, transparency, and kindness.

3. I advocate and fight for fairness, justice, and equality.

The first one I have discussed in some detail above. The second and third, not yet. How I have been able to apply these principles in life and where I have tripped on the path, will no doubt emerge in the chapters to come.

# Youth

I started at Auckland University in March 1969. My first year as a student was a blast! There were no university fees, and I was paid a living allowance from the public purse. The economy was still in overdrive so future prospects seemed assured. I was enjoying my newfound independence, academic study, student activism, and the chance to explore new horizons, including love and sexuality. I was also heavily involved in Habonim and had become a *madrich* (group leader) co-responsible for a group of kids just a couple of years younger than me.

For most of my childhood, I had aspired to become an architect, so had always planned to enrol in a BArch. However, first-year Architecture at the time, a Foundation Year, comprised: Maths I, Physics I, Chemistry I and a selective fourth unit. In the matriculation exams, I had done extremely well in mathematics and physics but very poorly in chemistry, which was no surprise since I hated it with a passion. Such was my aversion to the subject, that I could not face doing it for another year, so I enrolled in a BSc instead, taking Maths II (exempted Maths I due to my matriculation grade), Physics I and Philosophy I.

The early '70s in NZ and Australia equated to the late '60s in the US. As Bob Dylan put it, "the times they were a-changin'." I consider it a great privilege to have been a rebellious youth at that particular point in history and an enthusiastic participant in a seminal movement for political, cultural, and social change. *Political* change would end the war in Vietnam, initiate the demise of apartheid in South Africa and eventually bring down the iron curtain. *Cultural* change in music, art, fashion, and lifestyles infiltrated western society. And *social* change, shaped by a growing awareness of all manner of discrimination and oppression in society, transformed values, beliefs, attitudes, and behaviours. I guess this was typified most clearly by the rise of feminism. It was an amazing time to be a youth with a radical streak. Having now reached my 70$^{th}$ year and just had a stroke, I can fully concur with a Facebook meme I saw today: "Being 20 in the '70s was much more fun than being 70 in the '20s."

It is funny how things work out. The following year, they dropped chemistry from the first year architecture course. However, I was living in Sydney by then and enjoying maths and philosophy so much, I would not have switched anyway. So instead of undertaking a very demanding five-year professional degree, I cruised through a much more spacious three-year course that allowed ample time for extra-circular fun and games. Had it not been for that quirk of fate, my life would almost certainly have unfolded very differently. I can only speculate that I would have knuckled down to the requisite study, graduated, entered the architecture profession, and never become a hippie raising my kids on a commune in northern NSW. So I am damned glad I chose differently. But, on second thought, had I entered the architecture course at Auckland Uni and transferred to Sydney a year later I probably would have been involved in organising the 1973 Nimbin Aquarius Festival in my final year of study. (The event organisers were predominantly senior architecture students from Sydney.) So who knows how things might have worked out?!

Anyway, I studied sufficiently hard in my first year to do well academically but still enjoy life to the max. I remember playing a *lot* of cards in the student common room – mostly poker and 500. And I dabbled in student politics, which in 1969, were led by an eccentric student radical named Tim Shadbolt. Shadbolt was a great orator; I recall hearing him speak at rallies in Albert Park, adjacent to the campus. He led the radical-left organisation, the Progressive Youth Movement and, according to Wikipedia, was arrested 33 times at political protests. The contested issues were all things unjust, but predominantly the war in Vietnam. Shadbolt went on to become Mayor of Auckland and, eventually, New Zealand's longest-serving politician. If you are interested, I recommend Googling Sir Tim, as he is now; he was *the* most remarkable NZ politician, ever. I also participated in such rallies but managed to avoid being arrested as this was just the beginning of my radicalisation.

I also fell in love for the first time. My girlfriend was a vivacious beauty, a little older than me and much more worldly. As my first lover, she taught me everything I then knew about lovemaking. Our relationship was wild and passionate, inducing a depth of feeling that I did not know was possible. It made life to this point seem like a pale imitation of the real thing and in that sense, was a real coming of age. However, our relationship was to last less than a year. It ended because she wanted more commitment than a 19-year-old was willing to give; at least that is how I remember it. As things turned out, my family relocated to Sydney due to dad's business arrangements and I had to choose whether to go with them or stay behind. I was enjoying all aspects of my life immensely, so initially decided to remain in Auckland. I moved into student digs in the city. But I was not yet ready for that level of independence. In the following months, I struggled with my finances and the dance of my relationship, so in the end, I left for Sydney, too.

# Youth

I lived with my family for a few months whilst I started at the University of NSW, transferring into a BSc with credit for my grades in Auckland. That meant I went directly into third-year maths whilst I continued with second-year philosophy and took electives in music and psychology. My family lived in Turramurra, a far northern suburb, and the university campus was in Randwick, south of the city centre. I commuted by train initially but when that proved too time-consuming, bought a motorbike. I owned a series of bikes in those days – five, I think.

The next two years (1970-71) were hugely formative in terms of my values and worldview – a period of deep and enduring politicisation. Whilst I had been exploring political philosophy for some time as a teenager, the emerging horrors of both the war in Vietnam and apartheid in South Africa stirred something in me that has shaped my life, ever since. Foremost amongst my convictions, then until today, was a passionate anti-capitalism coupled with the belief that communal living is the most obvious and natural way for human beings to coexist. As a teen, the education that Habonim had provided, awakened the socialist in me. My radicalisation in Sydney awakened the Marxist. I will return to these ideas in chapters to come. But for now, I will stick with the storyline.

Within months I had joined Habonim in Sydney where I met and befriended a guy who would become a very close buddy and co-

## Youth

conspirator. Che (obviously, not his real name) was an impishly good-looking and charismatic card-carrying communist, i.e., a member of the Communist Party of Australia (CPA). He was not a student but, rather, a trade union organiser with a police record for organising illegal strikes and also anti-Vietnam war actions. The anti-war movement, which in good part was led by the unions, was way more militant in Australia than it had been in NZ. This was mostly due to the past five years of conscription, which sent unwilling young men to fight in Vietnam if they were unlucky enough to have their birth date drawn from a hat. I was incensed by the injustice of both the war and the draft, not least because I was eligible, myself, for the ballot. By 1970, draft resistance (i.e. refusal to register for the ballot) and draft-dodging (the burning of draft papers and/or refusal to comply) were well established. To engage more deeply with the cause, I joined an organisation called Resistance, which illegally abetted draftees to go underground either by heading for the hills (literally) or more commonly, moving to a secret safe house in Sydney. I was fully prepared to do one or the other myself, had my birth date of Dec 1st been drawn from the hat. As it was, Nov 30th and Dec 2nd were both drawn, and I was spared the trouble.

Resistance was an anarchist political party – anti-war, anti-racist, and anti-capitalist, which suited me perfectly at the time; as it still would, now. The organisation is still going, remarkably, and now campaigns on social justice and environmental issues. Its original name was Society for the Cultivation of Rebellion Every Where (SCREW), which was changed to Resistance during the 1970 inaugural national conference, which I attended. I also participated in numerous meetings and events, handed out our newssheet on the streets, and supported draft-dodging activities.

Che shared a three-bedroom house in the inner-city suburb of Bronte. When a vacancy came up, I jumped at the chance to move in, not least because the long commute between home and Uni was tiresome and quite dangerous on a bike. The house (shown above, refurbished, but still with what was my bedroom window in the front) was a stone's throw from beautiful Bronte beach and a five-minute ride from the campus. It seemed heaven-sent. I shared with Che and Robert, also a student – nice guy but very conservative. He eventually moved out because he could not abide our illegal shenanigans, including the drug-taking. Not unreasonably, he thought it might jeopardise his career.

Our home was a typical student house of the period. Posters of Jimi and Janis adorned the walls (but, actually, the music I most vividly remember was Knights in White Satin by the Moody Blues being played at maximum volume). Our drugs of choice were marijuana, mostly, and LSD on special occasions. We hosted many a party and there were endless political debates around the kitchen table, at which we ate lots of bacon. Che's political party and mine were aligned on most issues but opposed on others. The CPA was still staunchly allied with Moscow whilst Resistance was fervently anti-authoritarian, which gave rise to many a meaty discussion. But we were certainly united against the war, participating together in the famous Moratorium marches of 1970 and '71 (pictured below) which at the time were the largest public demonstrations ever held in Australia.

# Youth

The police were pretty heavy-handed, I recall, wielding their batons unnecessarily. By then, the war was beginning to wind down, but I like to think that our collective acts of protest and resistance were a factor in it eventually ending in 1975 with the withdrawal of the US and its allies. The Australian draft ended in late 1972.

But that was only the start of our collaboration as activists. Che and I ramped up our militancy a couple of notches when it came to the 1971 anti-apartheid campaign against the touring South African rugby team. At the time, there was an international campaign by the Left to disrupt sporting tours from South Africa in an attempt to establish an international boycott. Sport was an important means by which apartheid was legitimised by the white supremacist regime. The selection of their national teams was based on race; they were devoid of black and brown players. The 1971 Springbok tour to Australia was famous for protests so fierce that an Australian sporting boycott was implemented soon after. No South African team ever toured there again until after apartheid ended in 1994. Che and I certainly did our bit for the cause.

The following story has seldom been told because I have been aware that a police file on our activities may still be open. I do not know what, if any, is the statute of limitations on terrorism in Australia. I suspect that there is none, meaning we could still be arrested and charged. Still, I would like to get the story off my chest. Having to conceal an aspect of one's past is not good for the soul. Or, in the words of Maya Angelou: "There is no agony like bearing an untold story inside of you."

The Springbok team was going to be in Sydney for two weeks in all, playing several games at the Sydney Cricket Ground (SCG). They were staying in a hotel not far from the ground. On the first day of their visit, Che and I attended a small demo outside the hotel. We noted that there was little security – just a couple of cops keeping a casual eye on things. We also noticed the openness and vulnerability of the hotel building. The ground-floor lobby was fully visible to the street through a single, large, plate-glass window.

That evening, we planned an action that we hoped would gain some valuable media coverage for the campaign. We waited until one or two in the morning when we suspected there would be no police presence at the hotel nor any guests likely to be in the lobby. I rode pillion on Che's motorbike with a couple of bricks in a shoulder bag. We first did a pass of the hotel to check that the coast was clear, and no one was in the lobby, then rode back again on the left-hand side of the road so that I could use my right arm to lob a brick through the front window. It went perfectly as planned, causing due damage and disruption but no harm to anyone. And we were well out of there before the cops arrived.

We went to survey the damage early the next day, only to find that the window had been replaced before we arrived. The event went unreported. So we did it again a couple of nights later as there was still no police presence. This time, there was a little press coverage, but minimal. We aborted our third attempt as private security had been posted throughout the night. And they had added mullions to the window, dividing it into several separate panes. So we abandoned that strategy and decided to do something more ambitious that would surely attract decent press coverage.

We knew that the South African Ambassador lived in a harbour-side mansion with a private jetty at the bottom of the garden. We ascertained upon inspection that he had a couple of launches, one large, the other small, tied up at the jetty. Furthermore, the house was not gated and there was easy access to the water down a path on one side. We planned to blow up the boats, figuring that if we could just set fire to them, their petrol tanks would do the rest.

Again, things went exactly to script. Having left our bikes in the next street, we arrived outside the house at three in the morning armed with a couple of bottles of petrol, matches and rags. After checking that nobody was sleeping onboard, we set fires in both boats and departed. We heard two very loud explosions just as we reached our bikes and were a good mile away before we heard police sirens. Press coverage the next day was spectacular.

## Youth

AUSTRALIA'S FIRST ACT OF TERRORISM was a headline in one paper.*

Che wanted to reap maximum publicity from the action, so he called a TV channel and offered to be interviewed. The man was nothing if not brazen! The interview went ahead with his identity disguised. We adopted a bogus name, the People's Liberation Army (PLA), in order to add drama and create a perceived threat of further actions. But our two-person 'army' had no such plan. We had achieved the coverage we sought and anyway needed to get busy with preparations to disrupt the upcoming rugby test.

Che was well known to police so immediately became a suspect. Yet they had no evidence to connect us to the crime. I have no idea why the police did not just subpoena the TV station. Nor do I know whether they suspected me except by association. But, for the following several weeks whilst the rugby tour continued, a police patrol car was stationed opposite our house. I assume they were noting our comings and goings, or perhaps they were just there to intimidate. The whole thing eventually blew over but not before the far-right-wing Queensland Premier, Joh Bjelke-Pettersen, declared a State of Emergency when the team toured there. I like to think that our efforts were a contributing factor.

---

* This was in fact, not the case. Some six months earlier the Soviet embassy in Canberra had been targeted with an ineffective bomb thrown over the security fence. Perhaps then, ours was Australia's first *successful* terrorist act.

That's me in the centre

The rugby tour continued as scheduled despite there being violent protests at every match, requiring a massive police mobilisation to provide high security and protect the Springboks. (Security measures at the Sydney and Brisbane matches are depicted below.) Public opinion shifted dramatically as the population were awakened to the reality of apartheid. The movement pushed the Australian Cricket Board to cancel an upcoming South African cricket tour with Chair Don Bradman declaring, "We will not play them until they choose a team on a non-racial basis." It was truly a watershed moment in Australian political history, not least because it also led to closer scrutiny of race relations at home. I suggest Googling the 1971 Australian rugby protests if you are interested in reading more.

## Youth

Throughout those two years of continuous protest, I also had a life. I was studying, of course, and engaging with Habonim, although not in a leadership role such as I had in Auckland. There was something about Habo which made getting to know people and forming friendships easy, even for me. I would experience it again in London, a few years later. It seemed a bit mysterious at the time but having now lived half of my adult life in community, I better understand the dynamics. Intentional communities, if they are to thrive, need to pro-actively encourage and nurture social cohesion. To this end, the successful ones organise a programme of activities with the specific purpose of deepening interpersonal and collective connection. These go way beyond the meetings necessary to run the organisation; they are mostly social, cultural, and in many communities including Findhorn, spiritual in nature. Habonim was, after all, preparing kids for life on kibbutz, so it incorporated many such activities: personal sharings, games, dancing, singing, parties, rituals, outings, etc. The whole idea was to create an atmosphere of connectedness and family – a mini-community. Even as an introvert (or perhaps, especially as one) I was able to be my authentic sociophobic self and yet still make connections and form friendships. I did not fall in love again during these two years. With everything else going on, I doubt whether I would have had the time for a serious love affair. But I did enjoy several casual relationships as I became increasingly gregarious and less intimidated by women. I built many strong friendships with Habo folk, including some that have endured until today.

Campus life was full-on in those days! Students were as much focussed on having fun as progressing academically. In this, we were ably abetted by the Student Union. I well recall one Union-organised event where a couple of hundred of us gathered on the quadrangle lawn outside the library to watch porn projected three stories high onto the side of the Engineering building (shown below).

Then there was Prank Week, when students were given licence to stage practical jokes all around the city. One time, we noticed a crew of road workers digging a large hole in a road near the campus. I plotted with others to go and tell them to expect a bunch of students dressed as policemen coming to prank them by claiming that the works contravened road regulations and that they would have to fill in the hole. Then we called the Police Department and told them that a bunch of students disguised as road workers were, as a prank, digging a hole in the middle of the road. Then we stood back and watched events unfold. Things got pretty heated for a while until they eventually figured it out and had a good laugh…as did we!

My studies went well. My love of, and fascination with, maths deepened, and I enjoyed philosophy greatly. I was drawn much more to pure maths than applied. In philosophy, I preferred logic and reason-related units to the more abstract or speculative ones. In final year, I was invited into honours (4$^{th}$ year) in pure maths and continued with third-year philosophy – a double major. I found considerable overlap between them. The two units, Philosophical Logic and Mathematical Logic covered much the same subject matter but with different nomenclature. I loved the unity in that.

On the occasion of the very last written exam of my degree, I somehow misread the schedule and showed up a day late.

# Youth

Discovering my mistake with horror, I went to see the professor, thinking that, at best, he would have to set me a new paper. (My classmates would have taken their papers away after sitting the day before so conceivably I might have seen a copy.) At worst, I guessed I might have had to repeat the unit the following year, which would have been a disaster. The honours classes were very small, just four or five of us. So professors and students knew each other well. He asked whether I had seen the paper and trusted me to answer honestly. Of course I had not, so he kindly suggested that I stay and sit it in his office. I was very grateful but still very shaken up. A week or two later when the results were posted, I was relieved to see that I had passed, though only just. I had finished bottom of the class. When I bumped into the professor sometime later, he told me with a smile that he could tell from my performance that I surely had not seen the paper beforehand. And so ended my first stanza of academic study – with a whimper. Little did I know at that point that I would return to university a decade and a half later and be continually enrolled in 15 more years of study, this time, of architecture. But that is a whole other story.

I have never actually used my mathematics degree directly. I guess the only job for which it prepared me was teaching, which was never a plan. But apart from that, I was too busy exploring the world over the next few years, and being a hippie after that, to contemplate any kind of career. However, I would say that I have *indirectly* used my training in logical thinking ever since. I watched a video on architectural education yesterday that included 'clear thinking' amongst the attributes of a successful architect. In that sense, my training in thinking logically has been of great benefit as an architect. It has been of equal benefit in my work as a project manager and also a conference organiser. Both pursuits are all about logistics. So for that, I am extremely grateful.

Within a few months of graduating, I flew from Sydney to Britain and, with four other Kiwi kids, travelled by road down through Europe to Israel, to live on kibbutz. I was not then, nor have ever been, a Zionist. I believed that the valid ideals of Zionism, i.e., self-determination for the Jewish people, had been fatally compromised in 1948 by the devastating consequences of the birth of the Israeli State for the Palestinian people. The ongoing expansion of the State through warfare in 1956 and 1967 had deepened this conviction, of course. Nonetheless, I thought I would give it a go, despite my ideological resistance! (I think that would be called cognitive dissonance, these days.) The three-month-long sojourn through Europe is a story told in the chapter titled, Journeys, so I will now pick up the narrative from our arrival in Israel.

Most of the five of us landed on Kibbutz Yizreel, near Afula in the centre of the country. I was to live there for almost a year –

one of the most memorable of my life. I fell deeply in love with the kibbutz concept and lifestyle, feeling that at last, I was living a lifes that aligned with my values. My sympathy for the Palestinian people was also reinforced at the time, through friendships I formed with a family living in Jenin, the northernmost town in the West Bank. Also a refugee camp, it was located just ten miles south of the kibbutz. I was, several times, invited to their home for coffee. This was the same town (and by then, a city) that was decimated by the Israeli army some 30 years later.

The circumstance of my leaving Kibbutz Yizreel is a story that will remain untold. Suffice to say that it was triggered by matters of the heart and was very painful. But also, I was ready for a little more global exploring. So I went to live in London with my good friend, Johnny, one of the band of five travellers. He and I shared a flat and worked together on building sites, taking advantage of the inflated wages and cultural offerings of the period. A few months in, however, we were shaken to the core by news from Israel. The Yom Kippur War of October 1973 had claimed the lives of two close friends from Kibbutz Yizreel. I felt drawn to return to Israel once the war was over to volunteer in support of the recovery effort. I went where I was sent, which happened to be Kibbutz Afikim, one of the largest and most established such settlements (40 years old at the time with about 2000 members). I worked at harvesting fresh dates, scaling up the palms and cutting fronds of ripe fruit with a machete, which I then lowered by rope – fun work for a fit young risk-taker such as I was. Whilst there, I met and fell in love with a young English volunteer, Helen, the second serious love of my life.

After three months, I returned to London to be with Helen. We dated whilst I flatted with friends that I met through Habonim UK. She still lived at home but was a strongly independent, high-spirited young drama student with her own car. We had a ball together. Within a few months, I had become close to several Habo *chaverim* (friends) who were planning to make aliyah to a new kibbutz on the Golan Heights, Mevo Hama. So, despite my love for Helen, I decided to join them and give kibbutz a third chance.

The year spent on Mevo Hama was rich, rewarding and complex; my heart and mind were as conflicted as ever in respect of living in Israel. Ultimately, I made a firm decision to leave Israel and give up on the possibility of aliyah. Whist I adored kibbutz life, I just could not reconcile my pacifist values with living in a country at war. And as a young Jew, after three years in the country, I was obliged to join the army. (Being a conscientious objector was not an option back then, although it is now.) But worse than that, even back then in the early '70s, I could see that neither the Palestinian injustices nor the continual state of war in the region would be resolved in my lifetime, perhaps even the lifetime of my children. And for sure, I did not want that for my presumed future kids. So I moved back to London to pick up with Helen.

We first moved into a shared house with sweet hippie friends and eventually to our own flat just off lively Westbourne Grove in Central London. Despite our poverty, we managed to have a great time socially and culturally, including participation at two Edinburgh Festivals where Helen performed with amateur drama groups. And our love deepened further, such that when it came time for me to leave, we planned for her to join me in Australia on completion of her studies some six months hence. That reunion never happened, for reasons that will become clear below. So my final memory of our time together became the parting at the airport when we both broke down in floods of tears.

Back in Oz, I resolved not to rejoin the mainstream, but rather, drop out and live communally perhaps in some rural location. My experience on kibbutz had confirmed what I had surmised through reading, reasoning, and discussion in the years prior to going to Israel. Namely, that communal living was perfect for me, personally, and the most natural lifestyle choice, perhaps innately so, for humans, generally. Although I did not realise it at the time, many more years of communal experience, research and writing would eventually turn my hunch into a proven conviction.

## Youth

I set about finding a community to join. An opportunity arose to join a fledgeling community on the Hawkesbury River, just north of Sydney. The property was so remote, access was only possible by boat and even then, only at high tide. I lived there for three or four months, enjoying a lifestyle in sync with the tides, before deciding that this was not for me.

I was aware of an upcoming festival being held in Canberra in December of that year, 1976. It was the inaugural Down to Earth ConFest – a gathering of like-minded alternative types. A generation of young people, my generation, disaffected by the Vietnam War and disillusioned by mainstream politics, were seeking alternative lifestyles based on self-determination, eco-awareness, and love. The Back to the Land Movement, as some called it, was gaining momentum. The ConFest was seen as a potential catalyst for the movement, much as the famous Nimbin Aquarius Festival had been some three years earlier. Perhaps there, I thought, I will find the right community to join. The day that I arrived at the Cotter River where the festival was being held just outside Canberra, was the day I met my future wife, Jane. It would herald the start of the next phase of my life.

# Family

The ConFest was a real homecoming for me in a social, perhaps even a spiritual, sense. For the first time since leaving kibbutz, I felt I was with 'my tribe' – a feeling of being wrapped in a soft warm blanket of social connection. This is, perhaps, the core of what draws me to communal living on a personal level (as opposed to the theoretical level described above). As a socially awkward introvert, I do not form relationships or make friends very easily. It takes time. But somehow, in a socially cohesive community, whether it be residential (like a kibbutz) or transitory (like a festival), my sense of alienation falls away. I spent the first day settling in with 10,000 other free-thinking seekers, hippies, freaks, radicals, drop-outs, travellers, students, and the like. We milled about on a beautiful tree-covered site with adjacent camping and its own swimming hole in the lazy Cotter River. There was live music, delicious vegetarian food, free massage, and nude swimming. The loose programme of events was slowly getting underway.

The festival had been conceived and shaped by left-wing Labor Party politician, Jim Cairns, a socialist intellectual and economist who had been a prominent Vietnam War protester some years earlier. His open invitation to the ConFest was widely distributed throughout Australia leading up to the event. I think it is worth including here in full because it set the tone for an event that would become such a huge point of inflection in my life.

> DOWN TO EARTH: A Shaping of Alternatives
> The Cotter A.C.T., December 10 - 14, 1976
>
> The purpose of the festival is to show the urgent need to SHAPE ALTERNATIVES NOW. Ways must be found because of the violent, acquisitive, alienated, industrial society which now poses a threat to survival. People have for centuries searched for equality and the right and ability to determine their own development. Individuals must accept responsibility for themselves. Personal happiness and equality, as much as a good society, depend upon self-realisation. The most vital factor today is a sense of true identity. This is lost because our identities are created by others - not by ourselves. The all-powerful externally created hegemony in this assumed-to-be-free society, and its internalised personal alienation, must be understood if self-realisation can be achieved.
>
> The starting point must be the "will to be the self which one truly is". There must be equality and effective individual participation in government and in every other group activity if self-realisation is to be achieved. The festival will be concerned with the search for the true nature of man and

woman. For many centuries, the belief that man is inherently bad has exercised tremendous influence. Because of this belief, individual needs are suppressed, and the result is that personal helplessness, lack of independence and the desire to be led are created. From infancy on people are trained to be self-denying, falsely modest, self-effacing, and mechanically obedient. They are taught to suppress or hide their natural feelings and energy.

Social ideology is governed by contradictory altruism, by guilt and by the inability to experience work and action as a pleasure. This results in tendencies towards violence. But it is not the basic natural need of people that has a destructive and hedonistic outcome - it is the result of the repression of basic natural need that is violent and destructive. The internal social crisis of today that results from these contradictions means that we must SHAPE THE ALTERNATIVES NOW. There is not just one alternative. The new society will be made up of the choices of multitudes of people - individuals and groups - who are determined to find a way out. No one can be excluded.

Sincerely, JIM CAIRNS

On the first evening, I was sitting with others in a circle around a campfire and struck up a conversation with an attractive young woman next to me; Jane was her name. We conversed freely for some time before she revealed that she had arrived earlier in the day with friends and now had no idea where their tent was. As it was getting late, I did the only decent thing and suggested, in the free-wheeling, generous spirit of the event, that she spend the night in my tent and find them again in the morning. And in that same spirit, she accepted.

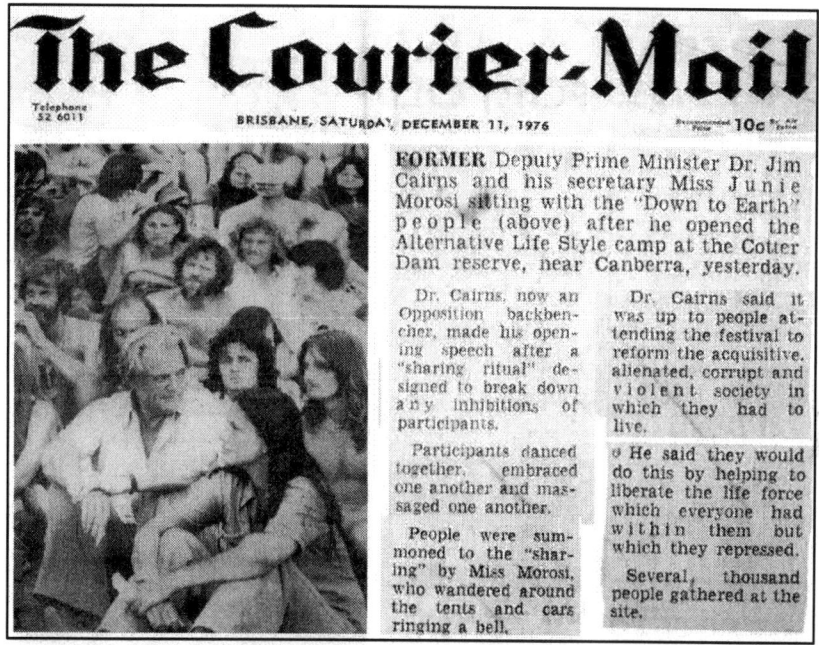

A newspaper report of the ConFest opening day

I have always felt that by far my greatest contribution to the making of a better, kinder, more compassionate world, has been my children. And although I am not a fatalist, I feel deep down that their coming into being was the principal reason why Jane and I met at that campfire. So in that sense, our seemingly accidental coming together was infused with deep meaning and purpose.

My intuitive 'knowing' that it was absolutely right, was reinforced by a remarkable story that Jane later told, which if I remember right, goes something like this. For a few years she had been a committed Vipassana Buddhist and for some time had been preparing for initiation as a monk. Shortly before the

# Family

ConFest, however, Jane had received a reading (Tarot, I believe) and was told that within 12 months, she would have a child and be living on a commune in some rural location. And, sure enough, that is exactly what came to pass.

Jane had been a law student at Queensland University and, following an internship, admitted to the Bar as one of the few female barristers in Queensland. But then she had seen the same 'light' as I had, deciding that this was not what she wanted to do with her life, and dropped out. She had come to the festival for much the same reason as me – in search of further direction.

Meeting and falling in love with Jane put an end to my plans with Helen, of course. She and I corresponded as friends for a while but then she seemed to drop out of sight. I briefly caught up with her shortly after moving to the UK in 2006, 30 years after that tearful farewell at the airport. She told me why she had disconnected from me, way back then. Helen had joined a spiritual cult (her description) called the Emin and retreated from the world. Later, she had left the cult, married, had a baby, divorced, and raised a daughter on her own. She had never realised her dream of becoming an actor.

Jane and I had a wonderful time at the ConFest and an even better one at a follow-up Healing Festival in a different rural location. The second event was more laid back and spacious than the first, allowing us the opportunity to relax, get to know each other and deepen our love. It became clear to us both that we were meant for partnership. We decided to seek a community to join together. Jane had a close friend, Sally, who was living at Tuntable Falls, a commune near the town of Nimbin in northern NSW. Nimbin had been the location of the iconic Aquarius Festival held three years prior. We knew that the event had spawned several new intentional communities in the region and thought that Tuntable might be a good place to begin our search.

We travelled north to Nimbin, then on to Tuntable Falls where Sally lived with her husband David. From memory, I think she was carrying their first child. We arrived late at night and were offered a bed in their curious but impressive handmade home. The next morning we awoke and gazed out through a large picture window overlooking Tuntable Valley. What we saw was wondrous and unforgettable, literally.

To this day, I can summon that vision from my rather dodgy long-term memory – of a long valley stretching away into the distance with dense rainforest along the ridges above and verdant green fields below. Misty white clouds were floating just above the valley floor. The morning bird call was cacophonous. It was like something from a mythical fairy tale. (The view below is not exactly the same one, nor is it as misty, but I think you get the idea.)

Family

We immediately decided to settle there and join the hamlet, Numenadi, where our friends lived – one of many housing clusters on the property. There was a vacant house site available nearby which David had intuitively cleared of lantana in the expectation that new neighbours, as yet unknown, would show up. We had little savings between us but could scrape together the joining fee of $200 each. Or rather, I think from memory we paid for one and deferred the other for the moment. In accordance with the community's building approval process, we raised a flagpole on the site to the intended height of the proposed home and, after a few days spent exploring the property and meeting folk, we went on our way. We travelled to meet Jane's family who lived not far away in Boonah, Queensland, then down to Sydney where my family lived. By the time we reached Sydney, we suspected we might be pregnant, so we were rather amused when my mother asked on the first evening, "Alright, now who is going to sleep upstairs and who, downstairs?"

# Family

We married soon after, in a simple but moving interfaith ceremony with our families at the famous Wayside Chapel in Sydney's Kings Cross. We planned to stay in Sydney with my folks for several more months in order to make enough money to build a simple timber house and whilst there, gather recycled construction materials for the purpose. I worked on building sites in one of the worst jobs I have ever had – cleaning brickwork with hydrochloric acid. We bought an old EH Holden ute for $35 and on weekends, scoured demolition yards for second-hand doors and windows. In those days, traditional leadlight was not much valued; we purchased beautiful stained glass doors and window for $5 or $10 apiece. Eventually, we headed back to Tuntable with our trusty ute overloaded with building materials such that close to home, the suspension collapsed, and the vehicle was rendered a write-off.

It was July 1977, just three or four months before our baby was due. We lived in an army tent whilst I built the first stage of our home and Jane prepared for a natural home birth. I recall drawing just one basic sketch plan of the proposed house but, mostly, I made it up as I went along. There was no time to do a proper set of plans or apply to Lismore Council for planning and building consent. I had no interest in doing so and, besides, nobody on the commune did in those days. (Most of us eventually applied retrospectively.)

Family

When I started building, I did not have a clue what I was doing. I can still recall on my first day onsite, embarrassingly having to ask my neighbour to show me how to drive a nail! As mentioned, Jane and I had foraged a ute load of recycled doors and windows whilst living in Sydney beforehand. We were also gifted some excellent building materials by Jane's dad, a successful machinery dealer, who had recently acquired and demolished an old timber road bridge. The 9 x 4s and 7 x 6s he donated were of ironbark (one of Australia's densest hardwoods) which, as the decking of the bridge, had been well maintained for over 100 years. They became the bearers and columns of the house. But they were like steel; nails had to be pre-drilled (which is why I needed advice from my neighbour) and drilling bolt holes through them became an epic task, consuming many days and several diamond-tipped drill bits. My father-in-law also offered us two pieces of assembled hardwood flooring sized 6m x 3m and 3m x 3m. When placed together, these determined the L-shaped interior layout; the former became the open living-dining-kitchen area and the latter, the bedroom. We filled in the missing quadrant with an open-sided veranda facing the

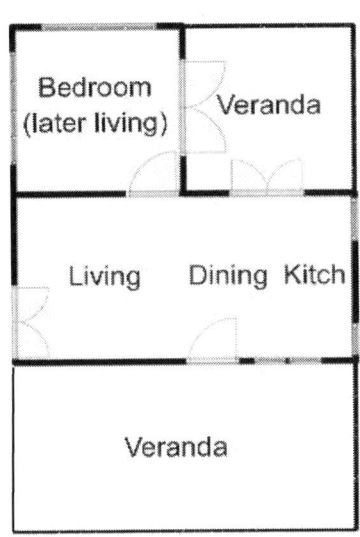

view down the valley and added another veranda all along the back. We then deployed our gorgeous, traditional, stained-glass doors and windows to best effect and, hey presto, the house designed itself; or rather, was designed around its constituent parts.

We installed a pre-loved Rayburn woodstove with back-boiler, built kitchen cupboards and a Coolgardie safe (a traditional Australian evaporative cooler) from off-cuts, and knocked up a dining table and bed base out of packing crates. The interior lining was cheap rough-sawn banana box wood. There was not yet a bathroom, so we showered with a hose and continued to use the composting toilet we had used since arriving on site. The water supply to the house came from a spring up the hill; light and power were provided by off-grid means. All in all, it was as affordable and ecological a home as one could imagine. The roof was a near flat skillion (mono-pitch) over the whole thing and the rooms were small, so the internal spatial qualities were unexciting. But it was *our* home, into which Jane and I had poured a lot of love, energy, and dedication. We had invested little capital, yet we owned it, debt-free. Well, that is not exactly true. Technically, all houses on the commune were owned by our governance body, the Tuntable Falls Coordination Cooperative, of which all residents were members (as were several hundred non-residential shareholders). Its rules did not allow for freehold or even leasehold private ownership (to limit property speculation and maintain housing affordability). However, we did own the right of occupancy which, in theory, could be sold on, should we decide to move.

Anyway, our home was beautiful, and we loved it. We moved in within a week of Jane's due date and Anna was born with total grace a few days later. It was a blissful, natural birth attended by the esteemed midwifery team, Carol and Norman. A few old and newfound friends from the commune and district were gathered on the veranda in support. It was a deeply profound, life-changing experience.

Life was simple in the days following. We just hung out together; me, Jane, and Anna. We had little we needed to do, nowhere we had to go, and not a worry in the world. It was a perfect welcome for our wee Possum, as we called her. That is us (below left) a week or two after the birth, with my family up on the veranda, (below right), making their first visit to the commune following the birth.

In addition to all the peace and love, Anna was also immersed in nature from day one. Our bedroom was supported on columns, 2.5 metres high. It opened directly on to the veranda (above right), which felt like it was floating amongst the eucalyptus trees growing along two sides of the house. For most of the year, we were able to keep the French doors between the bedroom and the veranda permanently open, thus blurring the distinction between inside and out. With wide windows along two of the other walls, there was little separating us from our natural surroundings. We were, of course, blessed with a benign subtropical climate, which in fact, made opening up the house to catch cooling breezes essential for most of the year. A decade later as an architecture student, I would gain a theoretical understanding of what I had intuited back then; namely, how to design for optimal comfort in different climatic conditions. Bioclimatic design, as it is called, would become one of my guiding principles as an architectural designer.

Early in the mornings, loud birdsong would welcome us to the day. Call and response between male and female Eastern Whip Birds were loud enough to startle even an adult, let alone a wee bairn. It is still my favourite bird call – piercing and powerful, yet smooth and melodious. And in the evening the cacophonous cicadas would sometimes be so deafeningly shrill that we would need to shut the doors on them. Then, there were the critters; possums and marsupial bush rats would visit by night, in good part because the food stored in the outdoor Coolgardie safe attracted them. Snakes were regular house guests too, mostly harmless carpet pythons but occasionally a more dangerous black, brown or tiger snake. And pademelons (small wallabies) regularly hopped about on our back lawn.

Anna, and later Liberty, were born into and grew up with this deeply intimate and completely natural connection with nature. Consequently, they had little fear of wildlife, and Jane and I tried hard not to pollute their trust with our own concerns. Even before she could walk, Liberty would visit the neighbours by crawling along a narrow bush track frequently traversed by death adders. Later, Anna adopted a pet leech, or rather a series of them, which she would carry around attached to her finger, often freaking out visitors. There were also domestic pets, of course: a rabbit, bantams, and more.

The opportunity for openness afforded by a subtropical climate would greatly inform the design of the third phase of the build. (I will come back to the second.) When Jane became pregnant again, it was clear that we would need more space; the bedroom was small even for the three of us, let alone four. (By choice, Anna, and later Liberty, slept in our bed for a good year or two.[*])

---

[*] Jane and I were heavily influenced by Jean Liedloff's seminal book, The Continuum Concept, which advocates maintaining close physical contact with babies 24/7 and for as long as possible.

Family

So we designed a two-bedroom extension to the north, not connected directly to the main house, but separated by a covered breezeway, which required passing through the outdoors when moving from one section to the other. Both rooms had generous cross-ventilation and the larger bedroom opened up fully to the north via massive folding French doors that were salvaged from a shopfront. We had enough of our recycled doors and windows left over to be able to beautify what otherwise would have been quite unadorned spaces.

Our second daughter, Liberty, was born in her own room in April of 1980. That is me above, in the main bedroom with Liberty shortly after her birth; the doors and one of the leadlight windows are behind me. Below is a basic plan of the completed house showing the different levels and phases of construction. The second phase unfolded during Anna's first year. We were always going to need a bathroom. Whilst we could manage with a compost loo and showering by hose, these were not long-term ablution solutions [alliteration intended].

With invaluable help from my brother, Alan, I set about building a bathroom and workshop into the open undercroft of the house. The space measured 6m x 3m, divided by columns into four bays, perfect for incorporating a 3m x 1.5m bathroom and 3m x 4.5m workshop. We began by pouring a slab, then built a full-height block wall along the back and a metre-high stone wall along the front. We topped the stonework with massive, recycled double-hung windows. Partitions, a tiled concrete shower-bath and toilet pedestal, a workbench made of railway sleepers and a septic tank, all followed. The whole thing was quite monumental, thinking back. But at the age of 30, being fit and strong with huge drive and motivation, no task seemed too big. Which is just as well, because a few years later, I launched into the fourth and final phase: adding another full storey on top of the original 6m x 6m section of the house.

In a way, this addition was a bit of a folly; we did not desperately need the extra space. After the two bedrooms were built, we removed the wall between the original bedroom and the living area, creating a more generous open living/dining/kitchen area – a kind of Great Room, in American parlance. And we could have settled for that. But I never liked the aesthetics of the near-flat skillion roof and had a niggling romanticised vision of what an attic space might be like. Removing the original roof and modifying the raked walls to level them up was tricky and had to be done fast whilst praying it would not rain; the whole living area was exposed to the weather. Again, I am surprised in retrospect that I even attempted such an operation. Once the new upper floor was in place it became easier to protect the level below with tarps. On top of the new platform, we built an A-framed roof that was about four metres high at the apex. Two large dormer windows went into the sides and a lovely ensemble of windows in the end wall provided a great view into and beyond the treetops. It was, indeed, a wonderful space that we used variously as a bedroom, guest room, yoga/meditation space and family room. But in fact, I am not sure that it ever got used enough to justify the trouble and expense it took to build. Below is the completed floor plan.

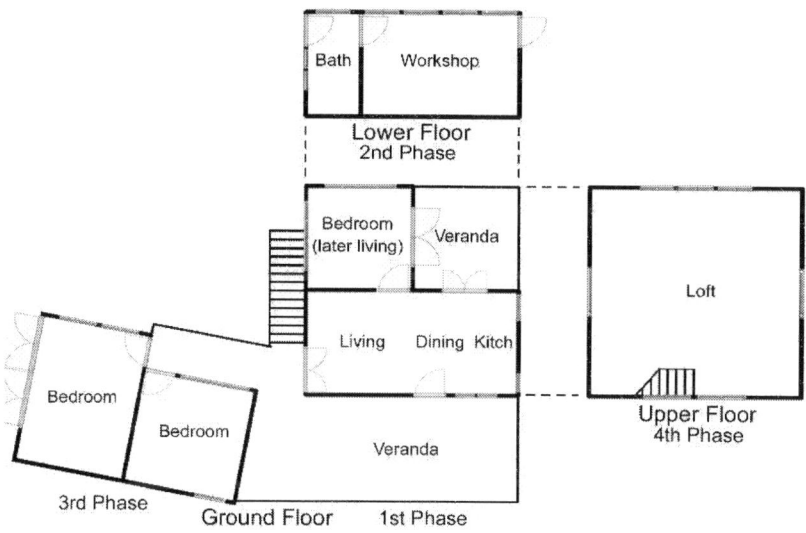

Family

This was for me, a period of deep fulfilment, wellbeing and the kind of contentment that comes with knowing that what one is doing is absolutely right, personally as well as 'politically.' The late '70s in Australia was a halcyon period of greatest New Age idealism. At the time, Nimbin was at the epicentre of the dream. We were, we believed, going to change the world by our example – an environmentally responsible community of communities, as self-sufficient as possible, materially, culturally, socially, and economically.

Alan, Jane, Anna, Liberty, and myself in late 1980

Living at Tuntable during this period cemented my belief that a nurturing extended family or 'tribe' is the ideal social grouping for the human species and that a socially cohesive group of individuals has the potential to be a profound milieu for the socialisation of both children and adults. Furthermore, an appropriately sized group, thus socialised, has the opportunity to create a truly civil society, one that nurtures grassroots action around shared interests, purpose, and values. I saw communal living as our best chance of fulfilling individual and collective potential for creativity, intelligence, compassion, and love – all those wonderful human attributes that sadly, for the most part, remain unfulfilled.

In addition to building the house, we planted extensive vegetable gardens and an orchard. Jane enjoyed fulfilling work as a midwife with the Nimbin Birth and Beyond team established by Carol and Norman. Life was busy, but we also took time as bona fide hippies to enjoy our freedom, swimming in the crystal clear Tuntable creek and hanging out in the sun with friends whilst playing music and smoking dope (moderately). The kids had a glorious life. From the time they could walk, they roamed as a pack with their peers, close to nature with minimal parental control but protected by the watchful eyes and loving attention of the one hundred or so surrogate mums and dads up and down the valley. In retrospect, Jane and I must have been very trusting or quite naive (or both) since seriously venomous snakes were commonplace. But I firmly believe that our girls benefited profoundly from the freedom, trust and love gifted them during their formative early years. Later on, they attended Tuntable's community school, which was another extremely nourishing experience for them both. Anna and Lib grew up to become secure, emotionally intelligent, and compassionate human beings. In their vocations as adults, they have sought to make a better, more humane world and to bring love and light to those in need. Their interests and proclivities took Anna into anthropology (working with aboriginal communities in Central Australia) and Lib into midwifery (working with underprivileged immigrant women in New Zealand). They have always gathered loyal and devoted friends and colleagues about them; through their being so loving, they inspire love in others. It is through this life experience with my kids that I have come to believe in the power of conscious conception, gestation, birthing and raising of children. I see it as critical to the making of empathetic, caring adults, who in turn, might build a more peaceful and loving world and a better future for the planet. (Some 30 years after leaving Nimbin, I co-convened a conference here in Findhorn titled, *Healthy Birth, Healthy Earth*, on this very theme.)

I went on to help others on the commune design and build their houses. Then in 1981, when the kids were about three and one, we went to the coast so that Alan and I could build a house for our parents at South Golden Beach. It was a kit home, delivered to site in parts. The logistics and problem-solving aspects of the build took me back to the pleasure I derived from playing with Meccano as a kid. The house was spacious, modern, and light-filled. Verandas all around faced out into what would become a dense tropical garden. The home, garden, and nearby beach, became a much-loved haven for my parents over the next three years until dad died of chronic heart disease, way too young at

# Family

the age of 63. Contributing in this way to Harry's peace and contentment in his final years was one of the most fulfilling things I ever did.

The home we rented during the build was sweetly located on a nearby river, but it had a nightmarish surprise in store for us. After we had been there a week or two, I discovered a loaded pistol in the top drawer of a low bedside table, presumably left there by our criminally negligent (or just plain criminal) landlord. The kids had been playing in the room since we arrived. I was as angry as I think I have ever been, took the thing and hurled it into the middle of the river. Our time there as a family was lovely in many ways but my memory of the home we rented is completely distorted by the shock and horror of that discovery.

Two years later, we lived in Byron Bay whilst I worked with my friend, Craig, on the largest building project I had worked on to date, a backpacker hostel called The Belongil Beachhouse. I was hired as a regular construction crew member but unexpectedly found myself in a new role. The design and documentation had been commissioned from a draftsman, not an architect – my first lesson in the difference between the two. The construction drawings were woefully inadequate; critical information was missing, and the dimensions did not add up. The design, as drawn, was just not buildable. As I seemed to be best on-site at reading construction drawings, I was drafted into a new role –

correcting, and completing the drawings, and then supervising the build. I became construction manager by default. The job went well, not least because we worked across the road from a beautiful surf beach and would take a dip in the waves when we began to tire in the afternoon. This boosted flagging energy and inspiration levels, enabling us to labour on for a couple more hours. Below are some recent images from the recently redecorated and dubiously renamed, Wake Up! Hostel.

During the build, we lived in a house just along the road that Craig and I built for his mum a year beforehand. The kids happily went to school and pre-school. We enjoyed beach and town life and slowly began to energetically detach from our Nimbin home and hippie lifestyle. And other thoughts and feelings were beginning to stir in me. I wondered whether I should not be paid more than bush carpenters' wages for the indispensable job I was doing. Further, my enjoyment of, and apparent penchant for, design, drawing and construction management, had reignited a long-held dream of becoming an architect. Without further qualifications, I could see that I would be trapped in the same kind of work I had been doing and never have a chance to fulfil any undiscovered potential I might have for architecture. So with Jane's blessing, I applied to several architecture schools and was accepted into both the University of Queensland in Brisbane and the University of Sydney. We opted for Brisbane because we would be closer to my mother who had moved there after dad died and also Jane's parents who lived in Boonah, about 90 minutes' drive away.

Jane's dad was again very supportive, this time buying us a house in a leafy suburban street, 100 metres from the campus. We felt blessed. It was also close to shops, schools, and public transport. We found a Montessori school for the kids that we felt had the same nurturing qualities as the Tuntable Community School and I began five years of full-time study expecting to become one of those 'barefoot architects' dedicated to environmental and/or community architecture. I thought that we might even return to Nimbin where I would set up such a practice.

The house was a basic, mid-century St. Lucia bungalow in original condition.[*] It was pokey, dark in places and had little

---

[*] St. Lucia is the name of the suburb, where such houses were ubiquitous.

connection to the outdoors. It required immediate improvement if we were to be comfortable: the kitchen needed modernising, the bathroom was inadequate, a separate toilet was accessible only via the kitchen, and I needed a study. So in my first two years as a student, we set about addressing these deficiencies: enlarging and refurbishing the kitchen; converting the smallest of the three bedrooms into a study; and extending out back to create a new bedroom, bathroom, and family/utility room. The family room remained open all along one side (so not securable) for another two years, in anticipation of a future deck. But at least we had a visual connection and ladder access to the park behind the house. Then over the following few years, we built a covered patio and carport in the front and a covered deck and meditation room out the back. A floor plan of the completed refurbishment is shown below with the original section of the house, shaded.

I had intended to describe the architectural ideas and qualities that we were able to inject into what was, originally, a very ordinary little house. But just yesterday, I came across a set of photographs that I think does that job better than words ever could. So I will let them do the talking.

The above shots show the lush tropical front garden that Jane created, as seen from the street, and the covered patio designed as a social space and also to integrate the house interior with the garden. The patio roof comprises polycarbonate sheeting, over battens, over strained cables supporting wisteria vines. The combination admitted generous natural light and dappled sunshine, which worked well for most of the year but could be too little protection in mid-summer. We installed French doors and windows along the front wall to give easy access to the patio and invite natural light, breezes, and views of the garden into the lounge and dining areas (shown above). The family room (below top left) opened up fully onto a covered back deck. The bedroom (below right) similarly had windows that allowed for maximum cross ventilation and views of the surrounding vegetation.

The deck and meditation room enjoyed views of the rear garden and park beyond. The roof was of polycarbonate over recycled adjustable louvres fixed in between rafters suspended from two beams flying over the top (visible in the right-hand photo). This unorthodox roofing configuration was tricky to construct but worth it for the way breezes, light and views flowed unimpeded through the space, whereas a more conventional supporting beam underneath the rafters would have had a blocking effect.

On moving to Byron Bay, then Brisbane, we rented out the Tuntable house but when it became clear that we were not returning, we decided to sell. As mentioned, we could only sell the right of occupancy, which monetarily was worth much less than even the materials it took to build the house, let alone the endless labour. So in the end we passed it on for a fraction of its real value. We were not overly regretful since we had known the rules all along. For me, the truly sad thing was how subsequent owners did not look after the place as we had done.

During these years, the kids were enjoying Montessori Primary and had adapted to city life pretty well. Not so Jane, however, who left behind deeply fulfilling work as a midwife in Nimbin and could not find an equally satisfying vocation in Brisbane despite completing a Masters in Community Health. I was fully engaged and thriving as a mature-age student, in good part due to a stable home life and the loving support of my family. I could not have done it without them.

I was doing well academically, and our refurbishment proved to be a valuable testing ground for my emerging architectural nous and confidence. The roof structures over the front pergola and back deck, for instance, were levels higher in sophistication than anything I had attempted before. However, I did become overly driven in my pursuit of academic success, oftentimes at cost to loved ones. I certainly could have been more present, aware, and responsive as a husband and father.

# Family

We did nonetheless enjoy a rich family life and that is what I now associate most with our St Lucia home. We were all foodies, so enjoyed both eating at home and dining out. Jane was always a great cook and Liberty, too, was showing early promise as a junior chef. We took many family holidays including camping almost every year at the Maleny, then Woodford, Folk Festival between Boxing Day and New Year. We binged on Brisbane's Expo '88 when the kids were about 10 and 8, taking a season ticket and visiting more times than I care to remember. And we regularly enjoyed weekends in Boonah with Jane's family including the many cousins of Anna and Liberty's age.

I continued to do well academically, graduating in 1990 with a high enough GPA to land a University Medal, just the third in the history of the department, I believe. I registered as an architect in the following year. When a vacancy as an architectural lecturer was advertised at QUT (Queensland University of Technology), I applied and was successful despite having limited experience of architectural practice and no familiarity with teaching. The medal swung it for me. So all the striving to achieve academically suddenly paid off in a way that I could never have predicted. It presented an opportunity to work in the profession as an architectural educator rather than a practitioner, i.e., for public good rather than private profit. Furthermore, my teaching remit was perfectly tailored to my environmental and socio-political interests. Candidate's backgrounds and personal interests were a factor in the appointment; the architecture school had nobody on staff with any interest in, or willingness to teach, sustainable and/or community design and the Head thought it was past time that these topics were addressed.

Enrolling in a part-time PhD was a condition of the appointment. I had six to eight years to complete it; whilst also undertaking a full-time lecturing load. It was a big ask, but one that was commonly demanded of lecturers in the '90s and ever since – a story that comprises a chapter (Research) in its own right.

Our home in St Lucia was fully refurbished by this time and, with the kids now in an excellent State high school, family life became all the more socially rich. We had all made close friends, so we hosted dinner parties regularly and celebrated birthdays and life events by throwing wonderful parties for friends and relatives. We were good at it I think; Jane and the girls were excellent caterers, and I was effective enough with logistics. With front and back outdoor covered areas, ours was a superb party house for a sub-tropical climate. And it was simply lovely to live in as a family. Meals on the front patio or the back deck were all the more delightful for their integration with the lush garden that Jane had created.

Our most memorable holidays, to my mind, were taken on the Great Barrier Reef. I think there were three separate occasions, but they were of a likeness, so I will write of them as one. Almost everyone knows that the Reef is one of the world's natural wonders. However, journeying there delivers a much more profound understanding, which comes via a visceral experience of deepest *awe*. We went to two different islands in the Bunker group at the lower end of the reef: Lady Musgrave (pictured below) and Northwest. Both are uninhabited and undeveloped but for composting toilets provided for campers. There is no freshwater, so absolutely everything must be taken over and of course, no trace left behind upon leaving. Camping is strictly controlled; a licence must be purchased at least a year in advance.

At QUT I made many dear friends. Amongst the dearest were two other academics, Jim and Adrian, whose company with their families made all the difference on these adventures, both practically and socially. They had more wild camping experience than us and were wonderfully convivial companions. We would set up a large, open-sided communal kitchen and social space under tarps and disperse our private tents amongst the ubiquitous Pisonia trees and Pandanus palms.

Snorkelling inside a calm, protected coral quay has got to be *the* single most memorable experience of nature that I have ever had the privilege to enjoy. For hours each day, we were transported to another realm – one of brightly coloured fish, curious turtles, gliding rays and docile reef sharks. Surely there can be no more immersive experience of an alternative reality, certainly not one as beautiful. The principal feeling was of wonderment, which I imagine could make a conservationist of even the most hardened heart.

And there were many more extraordinary natural phenomena to enjoy. On Northwest, we struck turtle spawning season. What a treat that was, especially for the kids. Watching those huge mama green turtles (and occasionally loggerheads or leatherbacks) lay their eggs late at night is an experience of deep intimacy guaranteed to turn impressionable children into lifelong nature lovers. And in the mornings, we would witness the previous season's hatchlings emerge from the sand and scuttle to the sea, which was wondrous to behold.

The birdlife on these islands is also amazing. Noddy terns nest in the trees in their millions whilst mutton birds blindly crash into campsites at night and make their burrows amongst the tree roots. All of these unique life forms are largely free from predators so show little fear, generously inviting humans into their world for a precious moment in time.

The kids' adolescence was, as far as we could tell, truly blessed. They fell in with a wonderful peer group of high school friends, which meant that they benefitted from all the right influences and we could generally be quite hands-off with our parenting. We had always been very permissive, of course, and had witnessed the benefit of that in their early development. So we saw no reason to change that stance. We knew that they smoked dope and given our background, could hardly object. Jane and I also still partook occasionally but tried to do so discretely. However, the issue was blown wide open when they came home early one evening to catch us red-handed. After that, we decided we might as well smoke together as separately, or better still, share a batch of the cookies that Liberty, in particular, baked spectacularly well.

I was doing quite some travelling during this period, both as a teacher taking students on field trips and as a PhD candidate conducting fieldwork. The story of the longest of these stints, a six-month-long residential in a Danish ecovillage, is told in the chapter titled, Research. We originally planned to go as a family, during which time, Jane and I would contribute to community life as volunteers whilst the kids attended school. (We assumed that at least some home-schooling would be necessary.) We were all ready to travel when Jane's mum was diagnosed with

# Family

aggressive cancer, so she and the kids had to stay behind, and I went alone, which proved to be fateful. Suffice to say that, due to a serious indiscretion on my part, it did not go well in terms of my relationship with Jane.

By the time I returned home, our marriage had fractured, and Jane and I temporarily separated for two or three months. Anna and Liberty were about 14 and 12. We eventually reconciled, and I moved back home. Jane and I stayed together for six or seven more years, which on the whole were loving and harmonious, as described above. But eventually, once the girls had reached their late teens, we separated again, and I moved out into an apartment in the city. It was the year 2000, my 50th.

Within a year, I had suffered serious burnout at work and quit with the aid of a timely early retirement offer. I was emotionally depleted, without work and needing to service a mortgage. And at about the same time, Jane and I divorced, rather acrimoniously. It was a period of enormous stress for us both, but particularly distressful for me as I was also estranged from my children for a period. I suffered a classic midlife crisis. But ultimately, as 'dark nights of the soul' are wont to be, it became a catalyst for deep personal transformation and triggered yet another radical change of direction in my life.

# Midlife

I began this new phase of my life living for five years in Fortitude Valley, Brisbane. The Valley had enjoyed a colourful history as a heavily trafficked working-class area where brothels and sex shops coexisted with low-cost housing, clubs, pubs, and Chinese restaurants. But being just a short walk from downtown, it was one of the first suburbs in Brisbane to become gentrified from the 1990s onward. Clubs, bars, and music venues were refurbished in modern styling, chic art galleries proliferated, and hundreds of up-market apartments were constructed. In the process, long-standing communities of residents were slowly forced out – a process in which, regrettably, I was complicit. I moved into a lovely unit there, which I will say more about in the chapter titled, Home. For a year, I commuted on foot to QUT along the edge of the Brisbane River. When I quit my lecturing job following burnout, I wondered what new line of work I might take on.

## Midlife

Going back into architectural practice was the most obvious option, but I was neither sufficiently resourced, nor much interested in, setting up my own practice; I am definitely not a businessman at heart. Nor was I keen to join someone else's practice. I had done this as an intern and become acutely aware of the unreasonable pressures and expectations to which staff are subjected in private commercial practice. And the burn-out had left me feeling very wary of taking on undue stress.

I decided to have a go at free-lance architectural photography. I had always been a keen photographer, first learning with dad's Box Brownie when aged eight or ten, then setting up a darkroom as a teenager and progressing on with a series of Pentax, Minolta and finally, Canon SLR bodies and lenses. I knew that I had a good eye, particularly for shooting buildings and landscapes, but was unsure that I could compete with long-standing professionals in the field. However at about that time (2001), the first affordable digital SLRs were becoming available and I could see that digital cameras made professional photography possible without the need of a dark room, or indeed, anything much more than camera, tripod, and computer. I had one distinct advantage over my competitors in the field. I was an architect, so could 'read' buildings better than many pro architectural photographers (of which there were only a few in Brisbane, anyway). And, I had lots of friends and colleagues in design practices, some of whom told me they had long been dissatisfied with the images they had commissioned from local professionals. They said they would be keen to use my services. So I bought a Canon D30 (which at three Megapixels was laughably low-res by today's standards), created a website and set about establishing my first, and last, business.

My 50cc scooter provided transportation for myself, camera, and tripod, plus occasionally an assistant. I would work on location two or three days a week, typically in the afternoons and evenings in order to catch the so-called 'golden hour' (when daylight is at its most conducive for shooting buildings) and two or three days at home in post-production, i.e. Photoshop, printing and burning media, delivering to clients, updating the website, and so on. I deeply loved the work; it was fun, creative and free-wheeling. I began to receive encouraging feedback from clients and also publishers who would sometimes reproduce my images in magazines. So at the end of my first year in the job, just for the experience, I entered the Queensland Professional Photography Awards, competing in the Commercial category with other architectural photographers as well as industrial, product and food photographers from throughout Queensland. I shall say more about that in the second last chapter.

Throughout most of this period, 2000-2004, Anna and Liberty were students at UQ and QUT, respectively. Anna studied anthropology and Liberty, film and TV. The challenges to my relationships with the girls that arose at the time Jane and I separated were resolved quite quickly and a loving connection re-established. They graduated and moved into their respective professions. Anna promptly relocated to Alice Springs as a government anthropologist, whilst Liberty took short term contracts in various locations, working mostly on reality TV shows (such as I'm a Celebrity, Get Me Out of Here). By this time, my mother and a new partner were gallivanting about the country in a Winnebago being 'grey nomads.' Essentially, all three of them had flown the coop, even my mum. Without loved ones living nearby, I was feeling much less attached to living in Brisbane. And after about four years in commercial photography, I was feeling that I had achieved about as much as I could, and learned the lessons available to me, given my limited resources. I would have had to invest in expensive high-end equipment if I were to progress. I was also over living in Fortitude Valley, which was beginning to sour as a residential precinct due to increased late-night street violence fuelled by drug and alcohol abuse. So I began to think about moving on.

An attractive opportunity arose that made effective use of my eco-architectural background and writing ability – compiling the building guidelines for a new ecovillage at Currumbin on the Gold Coast. Within a short time, I had signed a year-long contract, sold my unit, and rented another right on the beach at Tugun. Currumbin Ecovillage was the ambitious brainchild of developers, Chris and Kerry, with whom I worked closely. It was demanding work, but all the more satisfying for that. And although I did not realise it at the time, the gig was to prime me for the next period of my working life. By that time I had lived in Australia for about 30 years, yet never felt fully at home there. I was uncomfortable with many of its social, cultural, and political norms and attitudes. The preoccupation amongst Aussies with material wellbeing (e.g. the size of their house and model of their car) and lifestyle (leisure, holidays, and sport) were not what mattered most to me. And I believed it to be a fundamentally racist country. By 2005, federal politics was badly affecting my mental wellbeing. John Howard, an obsequious, conservative Prime Minister, had been in the role for about 10 years. He and his government of right-wing cronies had slowly been driving me mad. I reached a point where I hesitated to open a newspaper for fear of seeing yet another picture of him.

And at about this time, another feeling was building inside me. I was beginning to really miss living in community. I had not lived full-time in an intentional community since leaving Nimbin some 20 years earlier, although I had visited dozens as a researcher during the intervening years. And most recently, I had been a de facto member of the Currumbin Ecovillage. My love of communal living had never subsided. So I decided in mid-2005 to once again find a community to join, an impulse that knitted well with my deepening desire to escape Australia. I looked around the world and wondered where I might go. True to my instinct for research, I decided to make a grand tour of likely communities, visiting each for a week or two, participating in their induction programme, where they had one, and at the end of the trip, making a choice. It sounded simple. I sat down and drew up a shortlist of likely candidates, some of which I had visited before, others not. Shortlisting was based on certain criteria: size, age, culture, purpose and most important of all, economic structure. I was very keen to find a community which had, like the kibbutzim I had enjoyed so much in the '70s, an egalitarian economic structure whereby each member received the same remuneration irrespective of their role or position. I had never lost my socialist idealism.

The short-listed communities, in the order they were visited, were: Twin Oaks (Virginia, USA), Ganas (NYC, USA), ZEGG (Germany), Tamera (Portugal), and Findhorn (Scotland). I visited them during August and September of 2005, arriving in Findhorn in time to attend a major ecovillages conference, GEN+10. I had such an inspiring time at this event that I registered to do Experience Week, the Findhorn Foundation's introductory programme in the following week. About halfway through, on a crisp, brilliantly starlit night as I walked from the Park to Cluny,[*] having missed the last shuttle bus, I 'received' a

---

[*] The Park in Findhorn Village and Cluny in the nearby town of Forres are the Findhorn Foundation's two main campuses, separated by about five miles.

deep knowing that this was where I would now live. And that, in short, is how I came to live in the UK at Findhorn. It was a bonus that I could stay in the UK more easily than in any of the other countries. With a grandfather born in England, I was eligible for an Ancestry Visa and ultimately, permanent residency. This was how my brother, John, had settled in London in the 1980s.

Having made my choice (or perhaps had it made for me) I returned to Australia to wrap up my affairs, apply for the visa, pack my worldly possessions onto a single pallet, and return. I arrived back at Findhorn in March 2006, in time to commence the three-month-long Foundation Programme (FP), which at the time was how most Findhorn Foundation (FF) coworkers entered the organisation. I very much enjoyed and benefited from the programme, not least because I met Barbara (also a participant), who would become the fourth great love of my life.

At exactly the time FP finished, a crisis arose in the Foundation. An architectural project had gone awry, causing significant funds to be wasted. As there were no other architects on staff, I was called in to advise on certain contractual issues and as a result, the project was halted. Having saved the Foundation even greater financial losses, the value of my experience and qualifications were recognised and I was fast-tracked into a full-time position.

My working life in the FF has been divided roughly into two equal chunks. I was initially drafted into the Asset Development

Group, responsible for the design and construction of buildings and the installation of infrastructure. I remained there for six or seven years and was responsible as designer-project manager for several key projects. But at one point I moved sideways into an entirely different and quite new activity for me – conference organisation. I worked in the Conference Office of the FF for the next six or seven years, organising several large and successful events on important topics. Now in retirement, I volunteer in our Visitor Centre looking after the enquiries that come in by email plus organising and leading tours (although not during the lockdown, of course). I also do quite a lot of public relations work, hosting media folk researching for an article, book, or film. Yet, life in retirement is much more easy-paced and fluid. Having been obsessively achievement-driven whole my life, it is a joy to not quite be so preoccupied. It has been a revelation. I am much more relaxed, happier, and sleeping better, having been a chronic insomniac throughout my working life. I think I am a nicer person, too.

In some ways, I have felt like a bit of an alien in this community. I did not take readily to the more esoteric aspects of Findhorn's culture. I came in search of a socially satisfying, ecologically benign, community life, not to deepen a spiritual journey or communicate with nature spirits (the practices for which we are famous). So my personal take on the community, which fills the remainder of this chapter, is both a love letter and a critique. It is also a story of my growth and transformation as wrought by 'the magic of Findhorn.'*

The Findhorn Foundation Community (as it is commonly called), is otherwise known as the Findhorn Ecovillage and Spiritual Community or simply the Findhorn Community. I will probably shorten it further in this chapter to just, Findhorn, by which I will mean our intentional community, *not* the adjacent, 400-year-old traditional fishing village of that name. (Our use of *their* name is a contentious matter.)

It all began in November 1962, when the community's three founders, Eileen Caddy, Peter Caddy, and Dorothy Maclean first arrived in Findhorn with the Caddy's three children, Christopher, Jonathan, and David. It could perhaps be said that a mini-community began ten years earlier when the three came together to deepen their shared spiritual journey, which later was to become the foundation stone of the community. Their journey in spirituality, and also in life, was determined completely by the messages that Eileen channelled in meditation, which they believed came directly from God. In Peter's words, "during the previous ten years, every action of our lives had been directed by guidance from the voice of God within." † From the late 1950s

---
* This is a reference to Paul Hawken's popular book, The Magic of Findhorn (1976) which put the community on the map.
† From his autobiography, In Perfect Timing, which is a ripping yarn from beginning to end.

onward, they had been managing a large hotel and spa in Forres, not far from Findhorn. Day-to-day managerial decisions were based faithfully on Eileen's guidance, which was extremely specific, right down to the practicalities of who to hire and fire and which cutlery to purchase. And they were doing well; the hotel went from three stars to four and guest numbers were rising. But eventually, they fell out with the owners of the hotel chain who did not take kindly to their esoteric management style. To cut a long story short, they were fired with just three days' notice at the beginning of winter in '62.

And so it was, after life harshly dumped them in the Findhorn Bay Holiday Park (for want of somewhere better to go), that Eileen's guidance continued to shape every aspect and detail of their lives. Because they were flat broke, surviving only on Peter's unemployment benefit of £8 per week, they started a garden in which to grow food. Soon after, Dorothy also began to receive messages, which she attributed to the plant kingdom. She first contacted what she referred to as the *deva* or spirit of the garden pea, then went on to communicate with devas of many more plant species as well as elementals and unseen beings of different kinds. Most of these messages were practical – where, when and what to plant, how to do companion planting, how to make compost, etc. Peter would enact the guidance, developing the garden, seeking to 'co-create with the intelligence of nature,' as they perceived it. Soon enough they began to enjoy remarkable success, growing an abundance of oversized, healthy organic produce in very unlikely conditions – barren soil in a harsh environment. With the aid of modest publicity disseminated by Peter, visitors started arriving to see and hear what this was all about. Some of them stayed on. And, as they say, the rest is history. Even though the founders never intended or even imagined founding a community, one formed around them, and it grew, and it grew.

In the chapter, Values, I described a tripartite formula that I developed as a teenager for living a life based on fulfilling my potential in creativity, service, and love. This became my central objective or purpose. I think I have managed to carry that through pretty well, not least since I arrived in Findhorn, a community that embodies exactly these values.

Examples of Findhorn artwork that epitomise creativity, service, and love

Indeed, creativity, service and love are three main tenets of our spirituality. It could be said that our key mantra, 'work is love in action' synthesises these three aspects of the culture. We see all work as an act of *service*. We seek to bring *love* to everything we do by being fully present and engaged. And action, certainly as it was first modelled by Peter Caddy, is *creativity* made manifest.

Herein lies the source of the deep congruence and contentment I have felt living in Findhorn. Being a member of this community has enabled close alignment between my values and my lifestyle, which for me, is crucial to personal wellbeing. Furthermore, living here has enriched my daily life. It has provided practices, (which I will outline below) that enable me to further cultivate the abovementioned purpose. And as those practices have become second nature, so my contentment has progressively deepened. What is more, living in this community for 15 years has softened my worldview, a lot! Much of that change has occurred in the last seven or eight years. It took its time, but eventually, Findhorn worked its magic on my somewhat limited, sceptical, worldview – something for which I am extremely grateful.

There are three main strains to community life here in Findhorn: the spiritual, the cultural, and the ecological. As mentioned, the founding practices and principles were exclusively spiritual. The ecological impulse did not arrive for another 15 years, in the late '70s and early '80s, when environmentalism was gaining traction throughout the West. Since then, Findhorn has become equally famous as *both* a spiritual community *and* an ecovillage. The cultural dimension has existed since the late '60s when large numbers of vibrant, young creatives (predominantly American hippies) flocked to live here. Creative expression of every kind (art, music, song, dance, drama, etc.) has been a key ingredient of our community glue ever since, alongside the spiritual and ecological practices. These three strains are distinct, so I shall discuss them separately, but they also blend well to strengthen relationships and build the culture.

THE SPIRITUAL

Spirituality based on meditation was the foundation stone of the Findhorn community and it remains the most quintessential aspect of its culture. Yet, it is the one that I feel least qualified to write about. I am resistant because for most of my life I have been unable (and unwilling) to establish a spiritual practice, despite being surrounded by committed practitioners since childhood. My mother, Reva, meditated twice daily when I was a kid. For many years, she attended the School of Economic Science, also known as the School of Philosophy, a worldwide organisation with its headquarters in London. Its teachings are based on Advaita Vedanta, a branch of Hinduism as interpreted by founder Leon MacLaren (1910-1994). Mum and I have always been close. And she is a true inspiration in many ways – always calm, clear, and loving. But she could never get me to attend an introductory course, despite many invitations to do so. The organisation and their practices seemed just too inward-looking and esoteric for my taste, preoccupied as I was at the time with radical activism in the world.

My brother, John, did enter the organisation, however. He and his family have been deeply involved in the London chapter for decades. John is an inspiration – a successful professional in a particularly challenging field (corporate law), yet a wonderfully measured man with a calm and kindly disposition. I do not recall ever seeing him angry or upset. He has meditated twice a day, every day, for the last 40 years. Similarly, Jane, to whom I was married for 22 years, has always had a strong meditation practice. I fondly remember her attending a ten-day Theravāda Buddhist meditation retreat when our first child was just a few months old. I attended too, but as a babysitter. I spent each day wandering with Anna in a beautiful rainforest setting, presenting her for feeding whenever she was hungry. Later in life, Jane followed an Indian master, spending months at a time in his ashram in Northern India.

All of these people I love and respect and yet I never once took their example; I never seriously attempted a meditation practice. I remained unwilling, defiant even, about which I now feel a bit sheepish. However, after several years here in Findhorn, I eventually took the plunge. I was reaching a deeper level of contentment in life, which helped me access a level of inner stillness that supported spiritual exploration. I still struggle with meditation, however. Having always spent a lot of time in my head, simply stilling the mind is a real challenge. I have tried several techniques: focussing on the breath, repeating a mantra, counting, counting backwards, etc. They all seem to work for a period but after a few days or a week, they seem unable to prevent my mind from wandering off somewhere not particularly useful. And of course, I realise that cultivating patience and acceptance of whatever is going on is part of the practice. It is, as they say, the "journey, not the destination" that counts.

Currently, our meditation sanctuaries are closed. But for almost the entire history of the community, there have been two regular morning meditations in the Main Sanctuary (pictured above). At 6.30 the most dedicated members (and guests) sit in silence for an hour together. The more popular session occurs at 8.30 and is guided, i.e., someone will read a few lines of text or recite a short poem that might support those attending to take their meditation deeper. (I have been honoured with this role on a few occasions.) The collective element is also an important dimension. Sitting in stillness with up to 60 others, in a space that has been used for

## Midlife

the purpose for such a long time, is a powerful experience in and of itself. On the occasions that I attend, I am very much reminded of another core purpose of our community, which is to bring about personal and planetary transformation. This is nowhere better described than on a wee plaque in the lobby of the Sanctuary, one so modest that it goes unnoticed by many who walk past it to enter, squeezed as it is up against the fire extinguisher. It carries the words of Eileen Caddy.

> Why do we need time at the sanctuary? It is a place where we can come together collectively to consciously generate the energies of love, light, peace, joy, wisdom and divine power, which we do in silence. Then at the end, these energies can be sent out, not only to those around us or to the community alone, but to the world. This is where we become world servers and link to the 'network of light.'

A less visionary but equally vital purpose is ascribed to a related activity we call *attunement*. The concept was first developed at Findhorn in the 1970s by David Spangler, sometimes referred to as the fourth founder of our community. Attunement, he says, "requires a repatterning of one's inner state so as to align or connect with spirit. It involves shifting consciousness to allow greater sensitivity and openness to subtle phenomena."

In Findhorn, we utilise attunement many times during a normal working day. Almost every meeting starts with an attunement, intended to achieve an alignment in collective purpose. We may use it in a decision-making process to gain access to a deeper

## Midlife

truth than the facts alone reveal. Many Foundation staff begin a work shift with an attunement to bring themselves present and to connect with colleagues (illustrated below left, as held in the kitchen). We might use it to connect with particular qualities we wish to invoke for some purpose. Indeed, we use it almost any time we do something with purpose.

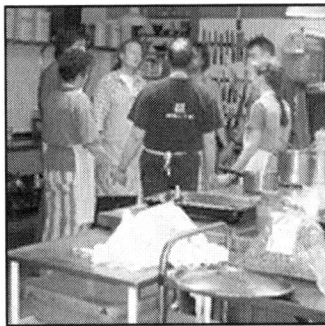 

An attunement is a mini-meditation of sorts. Someone will lead, asking the participants to close their eyes, soften their gaze or if indoors, focus on the ever-present candle in the centre. (We mostly do this sitting in a circle or standing with if outdoors.) Then, we might take a few deep breaths to bring ourselves present by leaving behind (mentally, emotionally, and psychically) whatever has been going on for us prior. Then the facilitator will lead an appropriate blessing, invocation, or visualisation, depending on the purpose of the gathering. Attunements vary widely, yet there is a commonality to them. Indeed, an experienced group does not need to be led, as such. They simply close their eyes and attune without a facilitator. The process can take between one and 15 minutes. I greatly value attunements and do not find them anywhere near as challenging as I do longer meditations. There is not sufficient time for the mind to wander.

I continue to be amazed by the way that input and inspiration comes to me in perfect timing. It has happened at least a dozen times during the writing of this book. For the last hour, for example, I attended one of the many variants of our attunement process called a 'leaving meditation.' And it happened just as I took a break at this precise point in the text. For some days now, I have been implementing proof-reading recommendations from my editor, Jane Ellen, who had kindly cast her expert eye over a draft. The last of her comments that I read before taking a break was, "Can you use a real example to illustrate the attunement process?" So here you are, Jane Ellen; this is how the leaving meditation went.

A leaving meditation is almost always held when someone leaves the Findhorn Foundation. Normally the participants would gather in person, in one of the sanctuaries. But this one was held via Zoom because we are still in lockdown. About 25 of us gathered to acknowledge and celebrate Ursula, a coworker who has just left her job in the Foundation and also moved out of the Park where she and her family have lived for many years. Ursula has taken many different jobs in her 15 or so years as a coworker (roughly the same length of time as me). Her most recent role has been in the Foundation's personnel department, known as S&PD (Spiritual and Personal Development), where she has been a mentor or 'supervisor' to many coworkers, including me.

The facilitator of the attunement, Eva, led a short (15 minute) meditation in which she led participants through a visualisation involving a metaphorical 'column of light' symbolising the 'energetic field' of the Foundation. I am sorry if this language is a bit esoteric for readers unfamiliar with the spiritual culture here. It *is* somewhat obtuse, which as you might imagine, took me many years to accept. Anyway, the visualisation involved Ursula "stepping out of the column of light," i.e., energetically leaving the Foundation. In response to this narrative, some people had strong visual experiences; I did not, which is normal for me.

When the meditation was over, we took turns to share what we 'saw' if anything, and also to express our gratitude for Ursula's role in our lives over the years, both through her work and on a personal level. And it was this 'sharing' which I found most remarkable about the whole event. I never fail to be amazed at how beautifully and skilfully my friends in the Foundation are able to express deep feelings of love and appreciation for each other. It is one of the great lessons I have learned here and has been a big part of my personal growth and spiritual journey.

Ursula for her part, was able to receive the adoration simply and openly without being overwhelmed or have it go to her head. That too, is something we learn in the Foundation, i.e., how to receive as well as offer expressions of love. I am in awe of the beauty of this process.

'Love in action' is a more diffused and widely practised spiritual modality than attunement. A shortening of the phrase, 'work is love in action,' attributed to Peter Caddy, it is a way of being whereby one brings full attention and devotion to whatever one is doing. In our work departments, where programme guests commonly spend several shifts a week, the concept takes particular significance. Before starting, guests are encouraged to go within, attune, and bring all of their attention to the task at hand, i.e., to 'do it with love.' It is said to be about honouring and connecting with the sacred within oneself and in all things.

Famously, once a year when the Maintenance team are stocktaking, some lucky guest will be offered the opportunity to count the screws…with love! And so it is with everything we do here. For me, this is a more effective spiritual practice than meditation. In a way, I think it is something that I have always done, i.e., been fully engaged with whatever I was doing. Bringing full attention, dedication and enthusiasm to my work has come naturally. I remember as a teenager, being riveted to a

TV series in which Bill Moyers interviewed Joseph Campbell about his life's work. I took to heart Campbell's encouragement to "follow your bliss." Generally, I have poor long-term recall, but I still carry a clear image of him sitting in an armchair and speaking those words directly to me, or so it seemed at the time. In retrospect, his advice might equally have been, "practice love in action."

Finally, there is one further aspect of our spirituality that is important to mention. *Openheartedness* is perhaps the most diffuse modality of all. Whilst the practices mentioned above, which we call 'inner work' (i.e., meditation, attunement, and love in action) are, essentially, tools for raising *inner* consciousness, openheartedness is about the *outward* expression of love. In all our relationships and connections we attempt to be as loving, kind, and compassionate as possible. This is not easy of course. People can be as judgemental and bitchy here as anywhere. But on balance, I think it is fair to say that this community maintains a high level of kindness, respect, and capacity for truly hearing each other. Engaging with such depth builds trust, which in turn, oils the wheels of collective process, which is essential to a well-functioning community, as described by José Luis Escorihuela:

> Friendship, caring, and mutual support: these are the qualities of human relationships that bind a community together. In an atmosphere of trust, communal processes flow with ease, laughter, and lots of fun. But trust needs to be cultivated. Trust

grows from deep heart-to-heart communication. If we allow ourselves to be seen by others authentically, with our weaknesses and strengths, if we speak our minds and hearts, trust naturally arises. A sense of group well-being is created.

It is often this aspect of our culture that most impacts our visitors – that sense of arriving 'home' that I mention elsewhere, of finding one's 'tribe' or 'family.' Over the years, I have heard many a visitor to Findhorn say that they felt 'truly heard' here, often for the first time in their life. By this, they mean far more than just being heard aurally. Rather, they have felt accepted and appreciated (loved, even) for who and what they are. This can be a primary catalyst for healing, which can also come to those who realise that they are not alone with their innermost thoughts and feelings, that their issues are universal. I personally believe in transparency for the sake of it. The more we humans can fully share what is going on for us 'privately,' then the greater can be our individual and collective healing and transformation.

THE CULTURAL

In normal circumstances, daily life in the community is packed with interest and richness, not least, culturally. We sing, dance, and perform regularly as a community in, for example: Sacred Dance sessions scheduled once or twice a week; regular open mike sessions (i.e., impromptu performances by musicians and poets); and occasional 'sharings' (variety shows of recitals, comedy, dance, etc.) performed by community members for each other. Plus, there is much that is spontaneous. The kitchen crew, for example, which before the lockdown included several folk from Spain and South America, frequently danced their way through a work shift.

Cultural expression is a key ingredient of the community glue here. We have both a visual art building, the Moray Art Centre (below left), and a performing arts complex, the Universal Hall (below right). The former runs a continuous programme of exhibitions and art classes whilst also offering studio space for artists to rent. The latter stages films, performances, gigs, and recitals, whilst also providing a venue for large meetings, conferences, and events.

I have chosen to write about the spiritual and cultural aspects of community life in different sections, but they are not separate and distinct. Creative expression, whether it be through art, singing, dancing, or whatever, can also be a spiritual pursuit. Let me illustrate with one of my most valued activities, which is also my most effective spiritual practice. Currently, it is being held online via Zoom, but previously, I would step out of the house every weekday morning at 8 am and walk to one of the best-loved and most photographed buildings in our community, the Nature Sanctuary (pictured below), famous world-over for its organic form and materials, as well as the beauty and symbolic power of its interior. This magical sacred space is home to one of our most well-established community practices. We call it *Taizé*.

Taizé is the name of a Christian monastery and residential community in central France where "kindness of heart and simplicity are at the centre of everything," wrote Brother Roger who established it shortly after WWII. Run by the Brothers, it attracts thousands of local and international visitors every year – people from many different backgrounds and faiths. They come in good part because of the style of worship, which is based on the singing of short simple songs, repeated time and time again much like a mantra. Indeed, the act of singing of these songs *is* a meditation, as explained on their website (www.taize.fr):

> Using just a few words they express a basic reality of faith, quickly grasped by the mind [and] sung over many times, this reality gradually penetrates the whole being. Meditative

> singing becomes a way of listening to God. It allows everyone to take part in a time of prayer together and to remain together in attentive waiting on God.

I find myself smiling at my choice of this quote. Over the years at Findhorn, I have slowly released my resistance to the use of the 'G-word'. Indeed I use it myself these days, but about an entirely different kind of god – the God within – that spark of 'divinity' within us all. This very Findhornian conceptualisation fits well with my humanistic worldview. It is shorthand, as I see it, for that potential we all have as human beings for the fullest expression of creativity, service, and love, amongst other things.

Taizé landed in Findhorn in the mid-1980s with the arrival of Barbara Swetina, a much-loved community songstress and musician who has lived here, on and off, ever since. She had just come from the Taizé community and was inspired. Another long-standing and deeply appreciated Findhorn community member, Ian Turnbull, had just finished building the Nature Sanctuary. Ian's sacred space seemed like a perfect match for Barbara's prayerful singing, so together, they initiated half-hour-long Taizé sessions that have continued in the same space, each weekday morning until recently (curtailed by the lockdown).

The sessions are facilitated by one of a dedicated group of leaders who set up the room, select the songs and lead the singing. Somewhere between 10 and 30 people attend, depending on the season and the number of guests we have visiting at the time. Most songs are sung in three or four-part harmony, so we sit grouped in voice parts: bass, tenor, alto and soprano. We begin by sounding three OMs. This is a way of bringing ourselves present, warming up our voices and somehow preparing the ground for 'spirit' to enter, i.e., for the participants to align with their essence, source, higher self, or inner divinity (pick your understanding). There are usually just four or five songs, each of which lasts about five minutes. The song itself is only a few lines long but is repeated ten or twenty times. The first song is usually a round, without voice parts but sprightly, requiring quite some focus and concentration. This will be followed by one or two more songs in harmonised voice parts. These are usually slower in pace and more meditative. They are simple, melodic, and generally quite beautiful. The lyrics are usually in Latin but there are also plenty of songs in different languages and from different religions and spiritual traditions.

Then, we spend a few minutes in prayerful silence. The leader will announce (for the benefit of newcomers) that, "prayers can be spoken out loud in any language or the silence of our hearts." I find this a particularly precious time of sharing what is important to us, and of being reminded of the universality of being human; no matter what our background, belief system, age, or education, we share a commonality of needs and wants, fears and concerns, dreams, and aspirations. Finally, we finish with an upbeat song that sends us out into the world with a smile and in my case, an earworm.

Taizé has been personally transformative in another way, for which I will be eternally grateful. I arrived in Findhorn believing that I was not, and would never be, a singer. I had spent a lifetime convinced that I was tone deaf. Even attending Taizé in the early days was challenging. But I have always loved listening to music, particularly choral singing. So I initially attended for the opportunity to listen in, and indeed, be immersed in some live, high-quality, choral singing. It did not take long for the music to weave its magic. Due simply to the nature of the songs – short, tuneful, repetitive, and easy to remember – I started to sing along, quietly at first. It took me a while and quite some practice before I gained confidence, but sure enough, the confidence came. And in what I perceived to be the non-judgemental atmosphere of the sessions, I started to sing louder and with more feeling. Soon I started to think that perhaps I could sing in tune, after all. And when I asked the experienced singers on either side of me, they assured me that I was in tune and that, in fact, I had a rich baritone singing voice. From there, I have never looked back. These days I sing without self-consciousness. And in so doing, I completely lose myself in the music. It has become for me, a genuine meditation – a means by which I access inner stillness, peace of mind and openness of heart, each and every morning. Such is the potential for personal growth and transformation in the practices we have here in Findhorn, as summarised by another quote from the Taizé website:

> Nothing can replace the beauty of human voices united in song. This beauty can give us a glimpse of 'heaven's joy on earth,' as Eastern Christians put it. And an inner life begins to blossom within us.

We are also a community that loves to dance. Normally, there are regular sessions, classes, and workshops of a variety of styles: 5Rhythms, Open Floor, Sacred Dance, Ceilidh and Biodanza; plus at least three other dance forms I can think of (Ecstatic Dance, Belly Dancing, and Contact Improvisation) that occur less often. All of these dance forms are celebrations of life, love, and the joy of being human. Now and again, we hold a dance party in our Community Centre which has an excellent sound system and mood lighting. And of course, there is dancing at private parties as well.

Sacred Dance has been strongly associated with Findhorn ever since the 1970s when Hungarian, Bernhard Wosien, introduced it to the community. He was a professional dancer and professor who collected traditional folk dances from throughout Europe, seeking to preserve traditions that were being lost. Those in Findhorn at the time recognised the deeper spiritual meaning of these dances and the practice took hold. It has been a strong feature of the culture ever since. We typically hold one or two sessions per week and include a taste of Sacred Dance in our introductory programme, Experience Week. I can still vividly recall the Sacred Dance session in my Experience Week some 15 years ago. We had our eyes closed for the final dance to extremely slow meditative music (Pachelbel's Canon, I think), starting in a widespread circle but magically ending up in a tightly clustered clump in the centre of the room. The feeling of oneness, of connection with others, stayed with me for days. The experience was a revelation, especially given that the last time I had done any folk dancing was as a reluctant primary school pupil. I hated it back then; I enjoy it immensely now.

I generally participate in Sacred Dance once a week during Sunday Taizé, which begins with one or two circle dances of a particular type. Known as Dances of Universal Peace, these are Sufi in origin, danced at a slow meditative pace. They involve singing or chanting by the participants and invariably induce strong feelings of connectedness and group harmony, joy, and peace. I also make a point of participating in our annual Festival of Sacred Dance (illustrated above). These week-long events attract dedicated dancers from around the world, some of whom have been attending regularly since the '70s.

Ceilidh, traditional Scottish dancing, is the third dance type that occurs regularly at Findhorn. The term, ceilidh, is derived from the Old Irish, céile, meaning companion. It is a traditional social gathering, common amongst Gaelic-speaking peoples of Ireland, Scotland, and parts of England. Ceilidh is an essential part of the community glue of these cultures. Traditionally, guests would play music, sing, and recite stories and poetry. Sometimes they would dance. This style of event continues, but in recent decades, dancing has dominated in most places. Ceilidhs are traditionally held in a community hall and occasionally on a smaller scale in houses and pubs. The music, usually provided by the likes of pipes, fiddle, flute, accordion, and drums, is cheerful and lively, as are the dances. The basic dance steps can be learned easily; instructions are provided for the uninitiated before the start of each dance. Here at Findhorn, ceilidhs are taught regularly and held on special occasions such as weddings and festivals, and at the conclusion of conferences, courses, and events. They are an opportunity for guests to learn something of our Gaelic culture and for all those attending to enjoy a congenial social gathering with old and newfound friends.

My journey with dance is not dissimilar to the one I have had with singing. I have spent most of my life feeling awkward and self-conscious when dancing, convinced that I was irredeemably poorly coordinated. But Findhorn has cured me! It took a while, but over the years as I have slowly been drawn into the dance culture, I have relaxed and opened to the joys of dancing. I believe that my journey of personal growth here is, in good part, due to the high quality of our social relationships: loving, trusting, and non-judgemental. In an atmosphere of trust amongst close friends, self-consciousness dissipates, leaving one fearless and free to challenge self-imposed limitations.

I would like to hand the last word on dance at Findhorn to my dear, recently deceased neighbour, Anna Barton, a long-time resident who was one of the forces behind Sacred Dance. These words of hers were written about Sacred Dance, but I think they equally apply to the entire gamut of dance offerings here:

> At Findhorn, the purpose is to enjoy dancing together in a non-competitive way, to learn that it is possible for everyone to dance together, young and old alike, to feel self-confident in a group that is supportive rather than critical and to be able to feel in contact with the earth, spirit, and each other. It is also used as a tool to channel healing energy for the planet.

## THE ECOLOGICAL

The essential characteristics of an ecovillage, according to the original 1991 definition by Robert and Diane Gilman, are that it be: human-scaled, full-featured, harmlessly integrated with nature, supportive of healthy human development, and sustainable. That is a bit of a mouthful, so let me take it one aspect at a time. *Human-scaled* means modestly sized so that the individual feels that they comfortably 'fit.' A village of any kind is generally no larger than a few thousand residents. In such a settlement, people know almost everyone, at least by sight. And the scale of building development is not overwhelming. *Full-featured* means that the settlement contains all of the features that enable its residents' needs and wants to be met – from housing and services to social, cultural, and economic needs. *Harmlessly integrated with nature* is a tall order. Few human settlements can claim that fully. So the idea is, to have the least possible negative impact on the environment. *Supportive of healthy human development* is perhaps obvious. *Sustainable*, on the other hand, is one of those words that means different things to different people. So I choose to use a dictionary definition: something is sustainable if it can continue indefinitely into the future.

By the definition above, Findhorn is one of the best-known ecovillages anywhere in the world, which is why we have been called "the mother of all ecovillages." There is no other human settlement in the Western world, of which I am aware, that better demonstrates all of the above-mentioned ecological attributes in its design, construction, and operation.

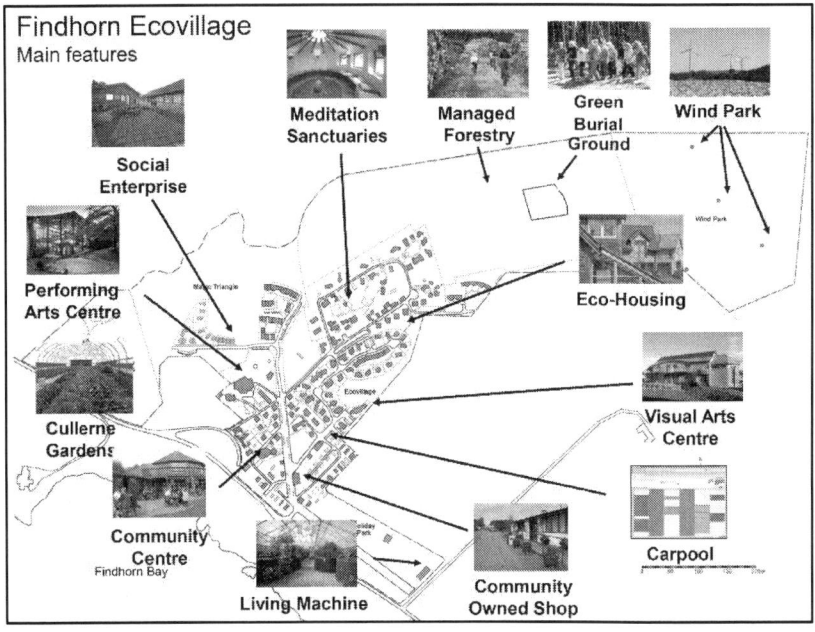

Findhorn Ecovillage (showing just some of its main features)

Findhorn has evolved an *integrated* ecovillage model that even goes beyond the definition above, incorporating numerous ecological, social, cultural, economic, and spiritual elements: several shared buildings including a Community Centre that normally serves organic, local, seasonal, vegetarian meals twice a day; performing and visual arts centres; eco-housing of many different types (attached, detached, tiny, mobile, straw, recycled, etc.); extensive gardens and a large food growing area; our own wind farm (below left) and numerous solar panels that between them generate roughly the amount of electricity we use; an onsite biological sewage treatment system called the Living Machine (below right); our own sustainably harvested woodland; a centralised woodchip boiler that distributes heat to more than a dozen community buildings; a carpool of electric and fuel efficient cars; a fair-trade shop that sells mostly organic produce and almost everything else that one might need; a comprehensive recycling systems including our 'Boutique,' a place to deposit and acquire used clothing, books and household items; our own community bank that funds affordable housing and numerous social enterprises; alternative health practitioners galore; a hot tub and sauna; several meditation sanctuaries; and even our own green burial ground.

We also have land and buildings elsewhere that render our range of resources even more comprehensive including Cluny (pictured below), a 100-room late Victorian building that was once a hotel and spa, located five miles from Findhorn, and a retreat house, Traigh Bhan, on the mythical West Coast Isle of Iona. On the island of Erraid, next to Iona, we have a satellite community of a dozen or so members as well as workshop and guest facilities. A fleet of shuttle busses transports members and guests between these locations. So by any measure, we deserve our reputation as a cutting edge example of a low-impact, integrated, sustainable human settlement.

What all of that means to me personally, apart from appreciating being part of such an inspiring project, is that it enables me to live a zero-carbon life, at least while I remain on site. (If I travel, that is a different story, of course.) And since I hardly ever need to go off site, that brings me tremendous joy and peace of mind. As I wrote above, living in Findhorn enables closer alignment between my values and my lifestyle, which for me, is crucial to my wellbeing.

# Research

The question from StoryWorth arriving into my Inbox this week was, "What was your longest project?" Yes, I thought, that is a worthwhile question. It allows me to write about my PhD, which in terms of the years it took, was by far my longest project. And it was also the most intellectually challenging, resulting in the greatest sense of satisfaction upon completion.

But upon reflection, I realised that I cannot write about my doctoral work without also mentioning the context into which it fits, i.e., my personal backstory, on one hand, and the aftermath of the project, on the other – indeed, all of my research, academic and otherwise, which in fact, is spread over my lifetime. So some of this chapter is personal but mostly, it describes the doctoral inquiry itself, and as such, may be a bit dry for some.

# Research

My academic research was the culmination of decades of musing about the value and importance of communal living. As I have already mentioned but will recap here, I first experienced the joy of communalism as a socially awkward teen of about 16. My induction then into the Jewish youth group Habonim, turned out to be life changing. For the first time, I felt that I could be my authentic self with my peers. I did not have to 'perform' in their company. Even as a shy introvert who hated being the focus of attention, I felt seen, heard, and respected. I felt that I had found my 'tribe.' And ever the social scientist, I was intrigued and curious, wondering what exactly was going on; what was it about the social and interpersonal dynamics of the group that induced this feeling in me?

At first, I thought it must be a Jewish thing. After all, according to the Biblical story, the ancient Jews were a nomadic tribe. Known as the Children of Israel, they were wandering Semites descended from Abraham. So perhaps, a sense of belonging to a tribe comes with the territory. Certainly, from the age of five when I started school, I was conscious of being different as a Jew – someone from an ethnic minority in a predominantly Christian, Anglo-Saxon culture. NZ and Australia are both fully multi-cultural these days, but they were not back in the 1950s. Whether it was real or imagined, I felt like an outsider (and was made to, at times, by the antisemitic abuse I suffered at school). But I also wondered whether the tribalism I was feeling at Habo was more universal than that. I reasoned that homo sapiens were hunter-gatherers on the African plains, not that long ago in evolutionary terms. And in fact, we continued to live fully interdependently in villages and towns, even in cities, for millennia after that, right up until the industrial revolution some 300 years ago. I have always thought that the pervading malaise of alienation and maladjustment that afflicts humans today is primarily due to the demise of that very thing – interdependency and mutuality. So perhaps my feeling of being back with my tribe was some kind of ancient limbic response.

But what I observed in Habo itself provided the best explanation. There was an ambient level of kindness and acceptance amongst members that was quite different from my experience of the world. Mainstream attitudes and behaviours in Australia and NZ, particularly amongst males, can be pretty harsh (more so in Australia than NZ, I believe). My Habonim experience felt like a cultural difference, and I bathed in it. And there was also a political difference. Habonim was a socialist organisation with the objective to prepare kids for life on kibbutz. In fact, it was and still is, a subsidiary of the kibbutz movement. Kibbutz in those days was fully socialist in the most fundamental sense, encapsulated in the famous decree by Karl Marx, "From each according to their ability, to each according to their needs." This referred to an individual's role in the collective and the fair distribution of goods, services, and capital. To me, the phrase also carried a deeper meaning – that at some fundamental level, we are all equal as human beings and deserve to be treated with the same dignity, respect, and natural justice. If you have read the chapter on my youth, you will know how passionately I applied this conviction in opposing both apartheid and the Vietnam war, two examples of terribly unjust oppression of the defenceless by the powerful.

So all of this was bubbling in me as a youngster, and when I did eventually get to kibbutz at the age of 21, I had a visceral feeling similar to my experience of Habo, namely, that I had arrived 'home.' The year that I spent on Kibbutz Yizreel was one of the most contented and fulfilling of my adult life. It confirmed in practice, what I had inculcated in theory through reading. The 300 members were all treated more or less equally, no matter whether they were in management or the toilet cleaning crew, they were all allocated the same standard of housing, received the same allowance, ate lunch and dinner together in the *chadar ochel* (communal dining room) and drove vehicles from the one carpool (there was no private car ownership). They all did a weekly KP shift (dishwashing) and they all had a single vote at the monthly general assembly. Kibbutz back then was probably the purest and most faithful application of socialist-Marxist principles anywhere in the world. My experience of kibbutz cemented what has become a life-long belief in, and advocacy for, communal living, especially where fundamental socialist

# Research

principles are adhered to.* But even when they are not, I see intentional communities as a vital and viable lifestyle alternative to overly individualistic and privatised mainstream society.

In the late '70s, by which time I was living in Nimbin, awareness of environmental degradation and global warming had become widespread. In direct response, a good part of our raison d'être as hippies on the commune was to live with low environmental impact and in harmony with nature. Respecting and protecting nature seemed obvious as we were surrounded by wondrous subtropical, natural beauty and we were all tree huggers at heart. Living amongst us were many experts on the topic who informed and inspired the rest of us.

---

* Sadly, kibbutzim underwent a financial crisis through the 80s and 90s causing most of them to privatise to some degree. Not so, Kibbutz Yizreel, however. Its systems and institutions are all still very much intact.

## Research

This proved its worth when, in 1979, led by conservationists Hugh and Nan Nicholson, the community mounted Australia's first-ever protest action against the wilful destruction of nature – a blockade to halt logging of old-growth forest at nearby Terania Creek (depicted above by photographer David Kemp). After a protracted and fractious stand-off between hippies, loggers and police, the NSW Government eventually stepped in to halt the logging. We were also anti-consumerist (by definition, as hippies) and supported each other in multiple ways to lower our personal and collective ecological footprint by building low-impact homes, producing our own organic food, sharing resources, generating renewable energy, building an alternative local economy and culture, and so on. All this, too, came easily and naturally.

This experience of life in community and the way it facilitated low-impact living, again got me musing about the whys and wherefores. It seemed clear to me at the time that communalism and environmentalism were a natural fit, but the underlying reasons were not so obvious. Anyway, I just got on with life, which soon enough plucked us from our Nimbin bubble and plonked us down in Brisbane, not into the mainstream exactly but another bubble – the ivory tower of academia and a privileged lifestyle in leafy suburbia. I imagined at first that we would return to Nimbin or somewhere like it, if and when I succeeded in architecture, and that I would become a community architect

## Research

designing sustainable homes and shared facilities. With that in mind and also because of my general interest in such things, I chose to write an undergraduate thesis on the topic. Titled *Architecture and the Ecological Crisis*, it was my first real opportunity to develop a more theoretical basis for the musings I had developed both on kibbutz and in Nimbin. But it did not allow for any empirical fieldwork, which was what I really wanted to do.

Within two years, I had landed a job as a lecturer at QUT and enrolled as a PhD student in the School of Architecture at UQ where I had been an undergraduate, mostly because I had a good friend on staff there with an interest in the subject area who was eligible and willing to be my supervisor. However, the topic I was proposing did not necessarily relate to the discipline of architecture; it sat more comfortably within the social sciences or environmental studies. So I was asked to develop an architectural dimension to the study so that it could be seen as valuable to the School. In any case, the research I had in mind was always going to lean heavily on the social sciences so my supervisor, Greg, and I agreed that I needed a second supervisor from that field. I knew of a guy at Griffith University (the third university in Brisbane) who had conducted his doctoral fieldwork at Tuntable Falls; he was well known on the commune. Bill quickly agreed to come on board, motivated in part by there being few Australian researchers who had followed him into the field of communal studies, which was well-established elsewhere (particularly in the US, the UK, and Israel). Bill was on the Board of the ICSA (International Communal Studies Association), an organisation of academics plus a few independent researchers who studied intentional communities, both historical (for example, 19th century sectarian and utopian groups) and contemporary (hippie and other communities from the '60s onward). He knew the leading scholars in the field and their work, so having him in support was going to be of great benefit.

At that point, I had to nail down the topic more precisely. Rather than jump in with something half baked, I started by reading the literature in environmental studies and the social sciences. I found that, at the time (the early 1990s), there was considerable research being done into what motivates people to act responsibly toward the environment. Repeatedly in Western culture, there appeared to be a conundrum. When researchers went into the street and asked random passers-by, "Are you concerned about environmental degradation?" (of which, there had been a general awareness for over 20 years) roughly 80% responded that they were. And yet, when those same respondents were asked, "What, if anything, have you done about that recently, in terms of adjusting your lifestyle?" very few could say that they had done anything at all. They were not even doing the basics (recycling, driving less, using less plastic, etc.), let alone reducing their consumption. There seemed to be a disconnect between people's professed concern for the environment and their ability to translate it into behavioural change – a classic case of cognitive dissonance.

Most researchers surmised that this was due to a lack of information, or insufficient top-down support (such as the provision of recycling bins) or perhaps, the entitlement felt by middle-class Westerners to the 'good life,' as they perceived it. But having had the experience of seeing how behavioural change to reduce environmental impact came so easily in Nimbin, I thought there had to be more to it than that – a social dimension of some sort, which seemed to lack mention in the literature. This was exactly what I had been musing about for a long time, namely, whether social relationships, social satisfaction, or perhaps social milieu, significantly influenced environmental behaviour. Bingo! I had a topic.

## Research

However, I still had to find an architectural angle. In 1989, just three years earlier, two young American architects, Charles Durrett and Katie McCamant (husband and wife) had published a book titled *Cohousing: A Contemporary Approach to Housing Ourselves*, about an innovative housing form that they had researched in Denmark.[*] They claimed that cohousing provided "real answers for the increasing number of people who stop to look at where and how they live, and at their impact on the environment." Finding their book was a real *Eureka*! moment. After reading it and looking further into what were called *bofælleskaber* in Danish, I realised that cohousing could provide not just the architectural dimension I was looking for, but the entire focus of the study. I searched the academic databases and found absolutely nothing on the topic, not even a published paper, let alone a dissertation, indicating that this was a research topic just waiting to be pioneered.[†] So I set about designing a programme that would take me to Denmark to do the fieldwork. I negotiated some PDP (Professional Development Programme), which is paid time off for the purpose, and planned with Jane for

---

[*] Cohousing is a neighbourhood of mostly privately owned houses integrated with a range of shared facilities including a 'common house' containing a communal kitchen and dining room. Cars are kept to the edge of the site and open space is designed for social purposes. Residents manage the project themselves and organise a rich social life that includes common meals, typically two or three times a week. For a full description, I suggest Googling cohousing.

[†] Nothing had been published in English but there were a few papers written in Danish, Swedish and Dutch.

her and the kids to come too (which as I mentioned before, did not happen). I intended a six-month-long ethnographic study of a single Danish cohousing project and imagined that that would be sufficient fieldwork on which to build the thesis.

Whether or not the residents of a cohousing project constituted an intentional community seemed to be a moot point. McCamant and Durrett, authors of the book that soon became known as the cohousing 'bible,' seemed to deliberately avoid associating cohousing with the communities movement. They were keen to portray it as a mainstream suburban housing option with a pragmatic rather than an ideological purpose. I imagine they did so deliberately because they had established an architectural practice specialising in designing and developing cohousing in the US. Perhaps they thought that any link between cohousing and hippie communes or, heaven forbid, socialism, might be bad for business. However, for me to be able to use cohousing to link communalism and environmentalism I needed it to be patently communal. And there was enough to glean from their description of cohousing life in Denmark for me to be confident about that.

Using the list in McCamant and Durrett's book, I wrote to about 100 *bofælleskaber*, and received a welcoming response from about 20 communities. I selected *Økologisk Landsbysamfund* (ØLK) located in NW Zealand, about an hour and a half north of Copenhagen by train. My design and construction background swung it for us, I think, as they were in the middle of their building development phase.

Økosamfundet Dyssekilde, as it is now called, turned out to be more like what we now think of as an ecovillage, although they had planned the settlement as a series of discreet cohousing neighbourhoods. This did not affect the viability of the study; in fact, it enhanced it. The community proved to be a rich source of research material, which indeed confirmed that the group was genuinely communal, so would readily sit within the intentional communities frame. I worked each day as a labourer on a block of flats being built for elderly residents, (the large, white-roofed buildings on the left of the shot below) whilst also conducting research using participant observation, interviews, focus groups, photography, and data from their literature.

The train from Copenhagen ran hourly along the track at the top of the photo, stopping at the station in the top left corner (but only if requested of the conductor). The fields to the right produced a

# Research

limited amount of biodynamically grown food, whilst in the top right corner is their solitary wind generator. They processed their wastewater biologically, or at least some of it. At the time I was there, they owned the steading and gardens in the lower-left corner of the photograph. These were old farm buildings being converted to common facilities including shared dining room, guest rooms, laundry, workshops, art studios, etc.

Top: Farmhouse and steading (left) communal dining room (right)
Middle: Biological sewage treatment (left); train from Copenhagen (right).
Lower: hauling concrete (left); completed homes for the elderly (right).

## Research

Some years later they sold everything south of the road, which is what prompted the name change and marked a shift to a less communal model (not unlike most kibbutzim at the same time). In my investigation of the social dynamics of the group, I noted a divisive tension between the idealists who founded the place and the pragmatists who came later. I guess the latter won out.

The summer of '92 was a great time to be in Denmark; it had the best weather on record and the national team won the European Cup, so spirits were high throughout the land. Toward the end of the six months, I became focussed on how cohousing ideas and principles appeared to have infiltrated conventional housing development throughout Denmark. So I investigated three more *bofælleskaber*, twelve mainstream housing projects and a 'new town' of progressive social housing.

This proved to be a fruitful line of enquiry because even then, and more so since, cohousing has greatly informed and inspired Danish housing provision generally, such that all new projects now incorporate common facilities and car-free open space designed for social purposes. Two of them are illustrated above, each with a common house.

For personal reasons, I left Denmark prematurely and returned to Australia with barely enough research material to complete the project. I spent the next two or three years massaging the data and formulating my arguments. However, I reached a point where I realised that I did not have quite enough data, nor of the right type, to be able to conclusively substantiate a link between social satisfaction and environmental praxis, i.e., people making lifestyle changes in accordance with their ecological knowledge and values. This was partly due to the dysfunctional social dynamics of the community I had selected. The ethnographic methodology I used did not help either. The cross-comparison of several cohousing projects I had conducted towards the end of the trip appeared to offer a more fruitful line of enquiry. So ultimately, I agreed with my supervisors that the Danish fieldwork was useful only as a pilot study, not the basis of the research. More fieldwork would be required, incorporating systematic *quantitative* data gathering.

Such mid-stream changes of direction in the project, some of them fundamental, are not unusual in a PhD programme. In my particular case, they were always going to be likely, if not inevitable, given my choice of Grounded Theory as the meta-methodology. Grounded Theory asserts that the shape of the study should be 'grounded in' and emerge from the data, not based on some predetermined hypothesis. I like this approach; nothing is set in stone until it emerges fresh from the data. But it did mean that I could not be confident of a successful outcome at any point during the first six years of the project.

By the mid-1990s, cohousing had become established in North America, thanks mostly to the efforts of McCamant and Durrett. More than 20 projects were completed and several more were under construction or in development. I negotiated several more months of PDP to conduct a fresh round of fieldwork. In early 1996, I wrote to all 22 completed projects, seeking permission to visit for a few days to conduct research. Two declined and two more proved unsuitable, but the remaining 18 were welcoming. They were located in four far-flung pockets of North America: New England; the US Southwest; Northern California; and the Pacific Northwest together with BC, Canada. The most efficient means of conducting the fieldwork was to fly between these four regions and drive between the communities within them, enabling me to spend an average of four days in each. This time Jane was able to come for part of the time; we had a fabulous time, driving south from Denver through the amazing landscapes of Colorado, New Mexico, and Arizona.

At each community, I planned my arrival to coincide with a common meal and, in most cases, arranged to give a presentation

## Research

on the first night. This enabled me to introduce myself, explain the research, and offer something back in return for members' cooperation. And where I could, I joined a cooking or washing-up team. I conducted structured and unstructured interviews, a photo survey, reviewed their documentation, and distributed a survey to each household. I went back repeatedly to each home to pick up the completed surveys or remind them to please do it. In the end, I managed to gather about 400 surveys from 80% of the households in what was 80% of the existing cohousing in North America, so any analysis emerging from the data was guaranteed to be highly statistically significant. The work was intense, but I was driven and inspired by it. I could sense that I was harvesting a rich pool of data and that this was genuinely pioneering work – the only doctoral-level research on cohousing being done anywhere in the world. Furthermore, I knew that, despite cohousing being a niche housing type, it was mainstream enough to be attractive to vast numbers of people, and also influence conventional housing provision throughout the West, just as it had already done in Denmark (and Sweden and the Netherlands, for that matter).

I got back to Australia with a huge amount of quantitative and qualitative data, and importantly, fond memories and positive impressions of the cohousing I had visited. I was convinced that this was a housing option that was very much needed by middle-class folk in Western society who were dissatisfied with isolated suburban living and wanted more community in their lives. Fired up with enthusiasm, I knuckled down to some serious analysis and writing. I was halfway through my eight-year-long window and had not yet written much. Still without a concrete hypothesis, I set about coding the data to try to make sense of it, pulling out dominant themes and relationships.

Regionally varied cohousing in North America: North Vancouver (top), Sacramento and Seattle (middle), rural Massachusetts and rural BC (bottom)

## Research

I identified two linked aspects of cohousing life: 1) varying levels of social engagement and/or satisfaction and 2) the motivation and ability of residents to apply environmental awareness in practice, which I called effective environmentalism. I used the survey data to compare the eco-practices of cohousing residents before they had moved into cohousing with one, two, three, four and five years after (see below). I found a steady improvement and was able to link that to social cohesion with a highly significant statistical correlation. Into the argument, I wove elements of community psychology and empowerment theory to formulate a powerful theoretical model (next page), which along with the correlation were the elements of new knowledge that a PhD has to deliver. I am aware that I am skirting over quite a lot that needs more explanation, so if anyone reading this wants to know more, then please either get in touch or else get hold of a copy of my book, which I will describe below.

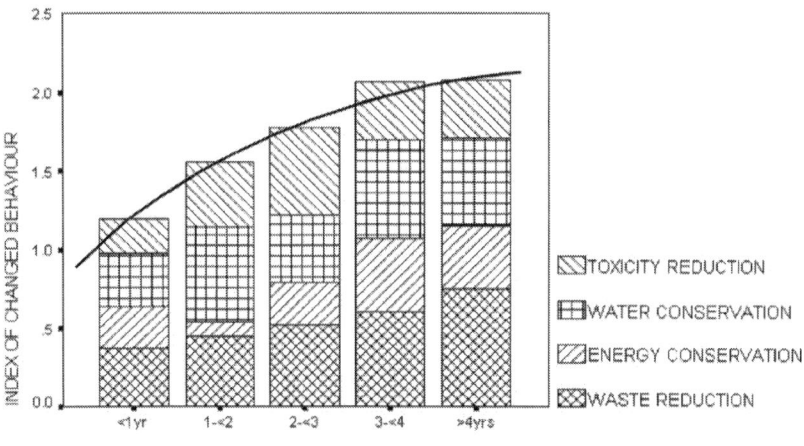

Research

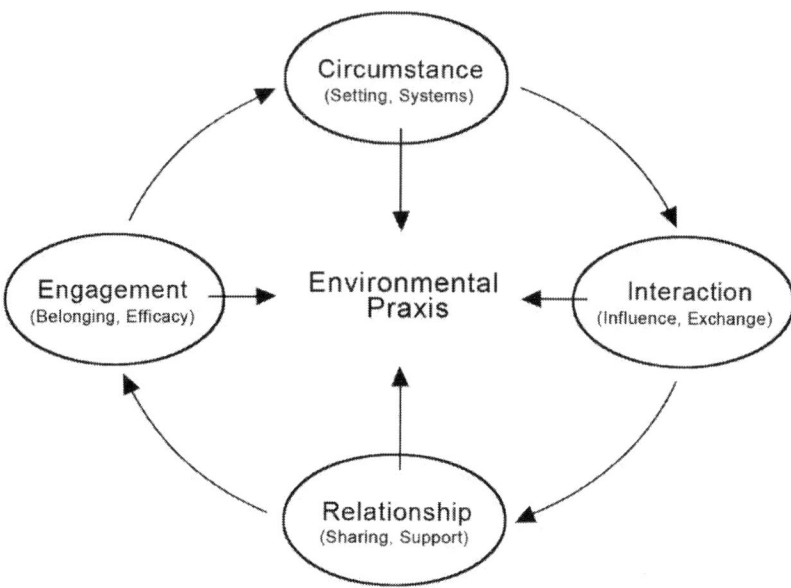

As I became increasingly confident that I was onto something and could make a genuine contribution to scholarship, I began to consider publication of some of the work. I started with a couple of modest papers in journals and presented at two Australian conferences and another in the US, the 1996 CSA (Communal Studies Association) event in Iowa. My first truly international conference came in 1998 in Amsterdam. Bill, my supervisor, encouraged me to present at the tri-annual conference of the ICSA. From what I could tell, ICSA members had not yet even heard about cohousing, let alone researched it or published anything on the topic. In fact, I gleaned from their literature, and also heard from Bill, that there was resistance to cohousing being considered a new type of intentional community, at all. I guessed that this was due to the housing being privately, rather than collectively, owned. I knew they were wrong about that and I was determined to set the record straight.

Attending the Amsterdam conference would set me on an unanticipated path for over 20 more years. I had imagined that my foray into the field of communal studies might begin and end with my doctoral work, but that was not to be. I had such a positive experience at the conference that I decided to join the ICSA. I very much enjoyed the scholars I met there, many of whom, like me, had once lived on communes or kibbutzim and turned to research and writing about them as academics. My paper was well received, and its publication in the conference proceedings marked the admission of cohousing into the lexicon of intentional community.

Back home, I still had a couple of years of intensive writing left to do, but it was going well, and I was enjoying the journey. However, things at work were not quite so rosy. I was feeling increasingly under pressure, being required to teach more and more students with a woefully insufficient budget for tutors. Domestically, life was also challenging, with Jane and I struggling in our relationship. Balancing all of these demands was taking its toll; I was feeling increasingly stressed.

But I managed to complete the dissertation on time and submit. It went to three examiners, one of whom had been a guru of mine over the years, Prof. Clare Cooper Marcus from UC, Berkeley. I was particularly keen to hear what she thought of it, not least because she was familiar with cohousing projects that I had researched in California. Months later I learned that I had passed, with high praise from all three and encouragement from Clare to publish a book based on the thesis but rewritten for a non-academic readership. Fortunately, UQ did not require me to also sit a viva, i.e., an oral examination, which was just as well; in my fragile state, I am not sure I would have been up to the task. At the graduation ceremony, I finally got to wear the floppy hat that Jane and I had joked was my main motivation for doing the thing. It was indeed very satisfying to complete and be able to call myself Dr Meltzer. For a few years, the title helped me get flight upgrades, but apart from that, I have seldom used it. Still, the satisfaction was mostly intrinsic. As a person who just loves a good project and has successfully completed many over the years, this one took the cake for challenge, complexity, and duration. It was my Mt. Everest of intellectual achievement.

But I was not done yet! Clare's encouragement to publish a more accessible book based on the thesis was something that I had wanted to do, anyway. It always seemed to me, quite tragic that many doctorates on matters of importance and interest to the general population were only ever read by other academics.[*] But

---

[*] Perhaps that has changed now that they are listed in accessible online databases. But before the Internet and Google, that was not an option.

if I were to do that, I would need a publisher (so I thought). I set out to find one, writing book proposals and sending them to publishing houses that might be interested – dozens of them! As I had the only PhD on cohousing, I thought that for a while at least (i.e., until the next one surfaced), I could call myself the world's leading expert on the topic; I hoped that might swing it for me. Even so, I knew it would not be easy, and sure enough, only one showed any interest, the prestigious University of California Press (UCP) based in Berkeley. They were keen to publish something about cohousing as they were located right where it was all happening; McCamant and Durrett had their practice in Berkey and several projects had been built in the area.

But there was a hitch – UCP's geographic focus at the time was the Pacific Rim and my research was focussed on European and North American case studies. So their editor requested that I expand the research to include more Pacific Rim countries. They would not make a contract with me, however, nor offer an advance to cover the cost of the additional fieldwork. However, I was keen to do the extra research anyway, as I wanted to engage with, and document, the cohousing activity beginning to unfold in my own back yard, i.e., the western Pacific where I had read cohousing projects were being built in Japan, Korea, Australia, and New Zealand. So I set about sourcing funding, mostly to cover the cost of travel to those countries. I wrote grant applications and sent them to likely funders – again, dozens of them! And again, I was successful with just one; I landed a US$6000 grant from the amusingly titled Graham Foundation, a US organisation that funds projects in the arts and architecture. I had included in the application, travel to the abovementioned countries and also to the West Coast of the US and Canada. The fieldwork I had done there before was now five years old and needed updating because cohousing development was unfolding so fast in that region.

Between semesters in mid-2001, I set out on a whirlwind trip around the Pacific Rim and also to Germany for a conference. It was an intense, compressed, and somewhat crazy trip. The conference was the next triannual event of the ICSA, which I had been involved in organising. Bill had been elected President at the 1998 Amsterdam conference and so it was his responsibility to organise the following one. He invited me to support him in the work, which I was happy to do. He had become a good friend by then; I enjoyed the Amsterdam event and the people I met there, so I was happy to support the organisation. Bill appointed me to the ICSA Board in recognition of my contribution and, I hoped, my worth as a communal scholar, which felt like a huge honour given I was so new to the field. (I could not have known at the time, but my role as assistant organiser presaged a future career in conference management here in Findhorn.)

# Research

ICSA conferences are almost always held in a communal setting – the site of a historical community long past, or a contemporary one. (The Amsterdam event, held at the University, was an exception.) Bill had controversially chosen to hold the 2001 conference at ZEGG, an established community in Brandenburg province of the old East Germany. The choice was contentious for two reasons. Many key ICSA members are Israelis whose focus is kibbutz research. As Jews, some of whom had lost family during WWII, many were reluctant to go to Germany. Secondly ZEGG is well-known for its radical approach to sexual relations, polyamory in particular, and this was confronting for some. But go they did, and the event was a great success, very much enjoyed by all. I presented a keynote address titled *Cohousing: Bringing Communalism to the World*, which I hoped would reinforce the legitimacy of cohousing as a new intentional community type. I also hoped to make the point that, unlike most, it was a communal model that could appeal to vast numbers of regular folk around the globe.

From there I headed back to the US and spent two or three days at each of the six or eight cohousing communities in California, Oregon, Washington, and British Columbia, most of which were new to me as they did not exist in 1996 when I did the PhD fieldwork. I stopped off in Auckland on the way home, to be able to include the only built project in NZ at the time, and then on to Hobart, Tasmania, where two more were up and running. Later that year, I visited Japan and Korea to document cohousing activity there, and so complete my circuit of Pacific Rim countries.

Back in Brisbane, I was feeling burned out by the teaching job, so left QUT at the end of that year. I was now reworking my thesis for a general readership as an unsupported, independent researcher, not a well-paid academic. I was also building a new vocation as a commercial photographer, so the book writing took a back seat for a while. By 2004, I had completed a manuscript titled *Sustainable Community: Learning from the cohousing model*. But there had been no communication with UCP for several years, so it was no surprise that they were no longer interested in publishing it. The editor with whom I negotiated had left the company and anyway, they had moved on from their focus on the Pacific Rim. I was pleased with the manuscript so was not going to let it sink for want of a publisher. Besides, publishing the book was a condition of the grant from the Graham Foundation.

Fortunately, by this time, a new digital technology had come to the fore – Print on Demand, or POD publishing, whereby a book is printed only when it is ordered. POD makes self-publishing way more viable as there is little upfront cost and there are no boxes of books that need to be stored and shipped one by one. I chose to use Trafford Press, based in North America which, for

## Research

a fee, offered some promotional support. And the book has been with them ever since (15 years now). It still sells in small quantities. I have had a lot of positive feedback about it over the years, mostly from cohousing groups that bought a copy and circulated it amongst their members during the development phase of their project. So it sits on a lot of library shelves in a lot of common houses, which more than justifies the effort it took.

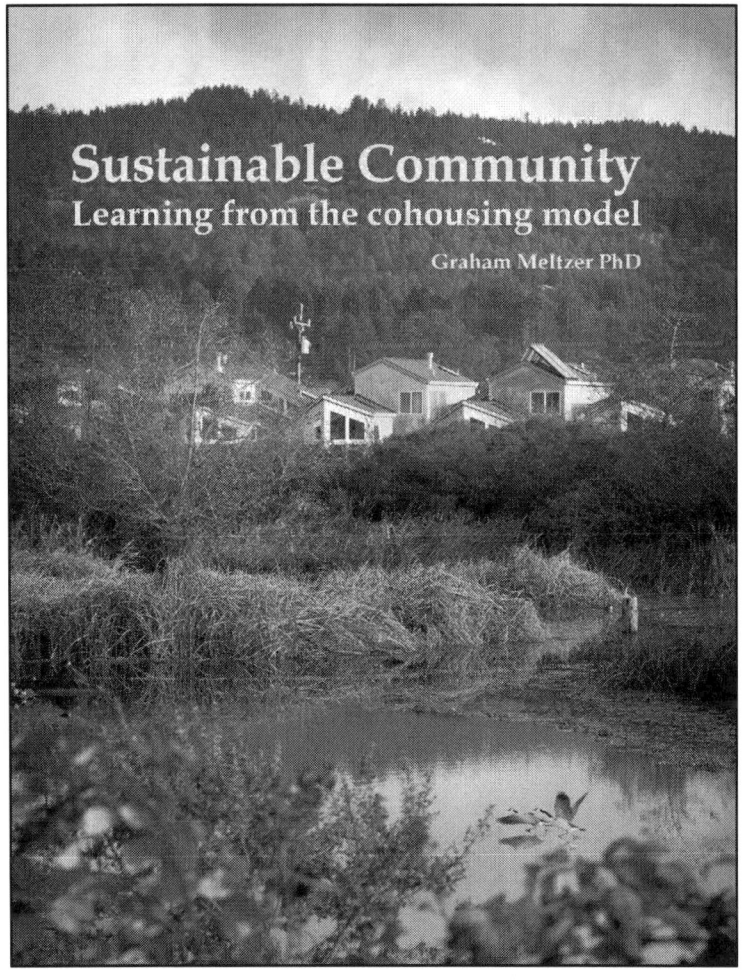

## Research

Further outcomes from the PhD project that I could never have anticipated include a 20-year journey on the Board of the ICSA, which led to yet another change of career path. I was not able to attend the conferences in 2004 (in the US) and 2007 (in Italy) so I desperately wanted to attend the 2010 event being held in Israel, not least because I was keen to return there for a visit. And having been at Findhorn for a few years by then and become familiar with the way our conferences were run, I fancied bringing the next (2013) event here. I pitched the idea to the Findhorn Foundation, and it was accepted. Then, in Israel, the ICSA Board met, as it always does at its conferences, to discuss possible venues for 2013. Again, I successfully pitched Findhorn (in competition with two other proposals) and agreed to lead the organisation of the event since the FF Conference Office would not be familiar with its unique format and rigorous academic requirements (including the vetting of paper proposals).

For two years, I worked on the programme and logistics in close collaboration with the next President of the ICSA, living in Norway, Jan Bang. I initially did so part-time, whilst still in my job as an architect. Then, a year out from the event, I joined the FF Conference Office, full-time. The event brought 180 delegates from 35 countries together with 100 or so Findhorn community members for a programme that was as scholastically engaging as ever, but because it was held in Findhorn, had all the added social and cultural richness that this community brings to its conferences. It was "the best ever," said some, hyperbolically. The Foundation was also pleased with the outcome, not least because it proved to be quite lucrative. My organisational and project managerial skills were recognised as worthy of retaining in the Conference Office, so that was where I served the FF for the next six years.

The conferences I co-convened during that time included: The *New Story Summit* (2014) about creating a new evolutionary paradigm; the *GEN+20 Summit* (2015), the 20$^{th}$ anniversary gathering of the Global Ecovillage Network; *Healthy Birth, Healthy Earth* (2016) about conscious conception, pregnancy, birth and early parenting; and *Climate Change & Consciousness*, (2019) about deeper level (including spiritual) responses to climate change. All of these and more made a significant contribution, I think, to the creation of a better world, and in those terms were amongst my most important ever projects. They were hard work, mind you – attended by 300-400 participants, which is the limit of our capacity, and hugely complex to organise. The last one, in particular, CCC19, was so demanding that I totally burned out in the process (again!) and was forced to retire as a result. But *Je ne regrette rien*. In a way, those conferences were a fitting conclusion to my 50-year-long vocational journey, based as it was on the precept I adopted as a teenager, to strive in this life to fulfil my potential for creativity, service, and love.

# Home

What is the deeper, symbolic meaning of 'home'? Clearly, there can be no *one* meaning or set of meanings. An igloo, a yurt and a McMansion are going to represent quite different things to an Inuit, a Mongol, and a pretentious Westerner. Symbolic meaning will always vary with culture, climate, location, and historical period. And something as subjective will be unique to each individual. My plan for this chapter to write about what 'home' has meant to me, which turns out to be a lot!

I am very much a homebody. However, I do not find it easy to describe exactly what I find so important about my home or why. The issues are deeply psychological and difficult to access. One clear reason, I would say, is due to my introverted nature, which often has me feeling awkward and out of place in the world. My home, then, has always represented a place of refuge or sanctuary

# Home

– a nest that is familiar, safe, and nurturing – somewhere I can authentically be my quiet, withdrawn self and not have to 'perform' as introverts often feel they need to do when in public.

---

Having struggled more than usual this morning to write the above two paragraphs, I just took a break and jumped on Facebook for a bit. With astounding synchronicity, its AI engine fed me the following piece by the Irish writer John O'Donohue; it expresses much the same thing as I intended, but way more eloquently.

### Where Love Has Lived

> A home is not simply a building; it is the shelter around the intimacy of a life. Coming in from the outside world and its rasp of force and usage, you relax and allow yourself to be who you are. The inner walls of a home are threaded with the textures of one's soul, a subtle weave of presences. If you could see your home through the lens of the soul, you would be surprised at the beauty concealed in the memory your home holds. When you enter some homes, you sense how the memories have seeped to the surface, infusing the aura of the place and deepening the tone of its presence. Where love has lived, a house still holds the warmth. Even the poorest home feels like a nest if love and tenderness dwell there.

---

Our home in St Helier's Bay, Auckland, where I lived between the ages of 9 and 18, had enormous significance in my life. It certainly worked well as a retreat from the world. It was remote from the road, quiet and cosy, and we kids each had our own bedroom. But the house meant much more to me than just that. It is well known that we are formatively shaped during childhood; our personalities, attitudes, behaviours, etc. are 90% established before we reach adolescence. And some of that shaping can be attributed to the buildings we inhabit, which in our privatised Western culture, primarily means our home (and secondarily, school, church, etc.). In the words of Winston Churchill, "We shape our buildings; thereafter, they shape us." The home of my late childhood, then, was the container in which family life played out. At a subconscious level I probably still associate the place with the loving feelings I have toward my parents and siblings: it is where mum made us yummy meals, night after night; dad played me his jazz records; Alan and I played cricket endlessly in the backyard; and where I would sometimes look after my younger siblings. These impressions are still strong in me despite being formed a lifetime ago. The house also imbued me with a deep appreciation of well-designed architecture, particularly the qualities of space and light, and the interplay of levels. I believe I have that home to thank for my love of fine architecture and for setting me on course to eventually become an architect.

The designer was Maurice Smith who had been an undergraduate architectural student in Auckland and a postgrad at MIT in Boston, studying with Buckminster Fuller and other luminaries. Whilst there, Smith embraced an unapologetically modernist design philosophy. After returning home in 1955, he designed a series of houses in Auckland that were revolutionary by local standards. Ours was one of the last before he returned to MIT where he taught for more than 40 years. Mum recalls that he struck her as being a bit of a hippie. And sure enough, back in the US in the early '60s, he came under the influence of the emerging counterculture, which transformed his design thinking. Smith developed a unique approach to architecture that he called 'friendly collage,' which encouraged his clients to bring their personalities to the design process and also participate in the construction. His own 'hippie house' outside Boston was a site of ongoing experimentation and alteration, as shown below.

The image is remarkably similar to my own final design project at architecture school in Brisbane, a multi-unit housing scheme, in which the hypothetical residents were encouraged to participate in the construction. Resident participation or owner-building has been a life-long preoccupation of mine, as has the utilisation of recycled materials, not to mention the healthy non-observance of building regulations. So perhaps, on some subconscious level, I was channelling Maurice Smith, having lived my formative years in a house that he designed.

The next home I lived in for more than just a short time, I built for my own family in Nimbin, NSW. As the container for our early family life together, it holds at least as much meaning as my childhood home, perhaps more. And to live in a house that one has created from scratch is, of course, a great joy in itself. The building feels like an extension of yourself; you know every stud, board, and nail, intimately, like the proverbial back of your hand. This would be the first of two houses that I would co-design, build and then live in, whilst a third received a serious makeover. These have easily been the most creative three projects of my life (building construction is, after all, sculpture writ large) and also the most rewarding given that I/we have inhabited them afterwards.

In summary, the symbolic meaning of our Nimbin home (for me) had two main layers. Firstly, it was the container for early family life, starting with the birth of our two girls – surely, the most emotionally powerful moments of my life. Then, seeing them grow up in a beautiful domestic environment that Jane and I created, surrounded by lush sub-tropical nature that Mother Nature provided, was profound and life-changing for us all.

Secondly, the design and construction of the home as an act of creativity and expression of love, was all the more transformative because I had not designed or built anything before. And although I could not have known it at the time, that experience as a hippie kicked off my professional career (nice irony, there), first as a bush carpenter helping others with their houses, which led me into architecture, which morphed into an academic career, which incorporated research of communities, which ultimately led me to Findhorn. Together, these two journeys (family and career) comprise much of the meaning in my life. My whole *sense of self* has, indeed, been shaped by both fatherhood and vocation. Personal meaning does not get much bigger than that!

After my third year of architectural studies, I took my 'year out' in practice as an intern with the esteemed architect, Geoffrey Pie, who had been a mentor to a whole generation of students and graduates. Geoffrey was a font of architectural wisdom, not least in his understanding of the deeper meaning of home. He won a national House of the Year Award for a beach home that was notable for its modesty, simplicity and sensitive integration with site and climate. I remember a similar project we worked on together, the George Logan House, designed for a client who was a paraplegic and keen scuba diver. We integrated a long shallow gutter into a horizontal awning over sliding doors between the living room and an outside deck. Clearstory windows ran all along the wall above the gutter. When a breeze rippled water lying in the gutter, sunlight would reflect off it, through the windows and up onto the raked ceiling of the lounge, generating a pattern reminiscent of the underwater view George might get as a diver looking up at the surface of the ocean. Such was Geoffrey's thoughtfulness and sensitivity to a client's soul; I learned a lot from that dear man. Which is just as well, because six months into the year, I received my first full commission – highly unusual for an undergrad just out of 3$^{rd}$ year.

A couple called out of the blue, saying they had searched without success for an architect who both designed for sustainability and would support them to construct the project themselves as owner-builders. Apparently, I had been recommended as a promising design student with exactly those interests and background. They wanted to build a three-bedroom house on their rural block in Upper Brookfield, west of Brisbane. The design brief was minimal: they had an art collection to accommodate and they "liked angles"! I was daunted but not deterred by the opportunity and over the next three months worked collaboratively with the clients, John and Sue, to develop the concept, do the drawings, and seek approval from Council. The design was somewhat geometric (in order to generate the angles) and it incorporated: precision orientation and consideration of sun angles; natural materials including mud bricks made on-site and sheep's wool insulation; extensive use of recycled materials; high thermal mass; passive climatic controls; and strong indoor-outdoor relationship from every room. John, also a bush carpenter (as well as an antique vehicle restorer and farmer), invited me to join him on the build and I, in turn, invited my brother, Alan. We dubbed ourselves the Brookfield Alternative Builders.

Top row: living room, kitchen, and hallway. Bottom row: ensuite and deck

The three of us laboured long and hard over the next three months through an extremely hot summer to complete the build before I had to return to Uni. The design-build process was hugely satisfying for both me and the clients, who have remained close friends ever since. I stayed with them many times over the years they were there, once for an extended period – yet another experience of living in a home I had designed and built. The feelings that arise in every case take a buried part of me back to being inside the cubbies I constructed from blankets as a small child. Is that about security, protection, familiarity, sovereignty, control? I am not sure; probably a blend of all of the above.

In Fourth Year, said to be the toughest, my mum asked me to design an addition to her house. On moving from South Golden beach after dad died, she had bought a traditional Queenslander (early 20$^{th}$-century timber house on columns) sited on steeply sloping land in Brisbane's Red Hill. Reva wanted a self-contained studio flat inserted into the vacuous undercroft. It is a standing industry joke that the first commission most architects receive is to design a house for their mother. Well, this was not quite that, but of course, I was delighted to help. Turns out that she eventually married one of her tenants, so my support with the design and build proved to be life-changing for her.

Following my fifth and final year of study, I worked as an intern for a year in a successful large practice in Brisbane, one with branch offices in several cities. The experience awakened me to the harsh realities of the architecture profession. Unlike Geoffrey Pie's, most practices are highly commercial in focus – profit-making engines partners who drive Porsches. My experience triggered a long-held loathing of the underlying relationship of exploitation between bosses and employees. I witnessed too many junior staff of that practice working 12-hour days for minimum wage (or less if they were an intern). That was the expectation and, as I learned, the norm in the profession. It caused me to rethink my aspirations as an architect. I just could not imagine myself as a career architect complicit in such a system. And as an anti-capitalist with zero interest in business, I was not drawn to the idea of starting my own practice, either.

A highlight of that year was receiving another private commission to design a house – a two-bedroom beach house on Coochiemudlo Island in Moreton Bay, Brisbane. My client was an 'interesting' guy – a wealthy retiree and dilettante who fancied himself as a patron of the arts, which fortunately meant that he gave me free rein to express my creativity. His brief was remarkably similar to John and Sue's. He wanted wall space for his books and art collection and he, too, "liked angles." The site was small, so it was necessary to go to two stories, which provided an opportunity to creatively integrate bookshelves into a stairwell. Again, a geometric design generated plenty of angles and resulted in a very pleasing outcome. He loved the house so much that when it burned down many years later, he rebuilt it exactly as before – a great endorsement, I would have thought.

When Jane and I separated in 1999 and I moved into Fortitude Valley, I was able to purchase a third-floor studio in a refurbished industrial building, just before values climbed steeply from about 2000 onward. Indeed, I was doubly fortunate in that it was the last unit in the project to sell, so the price was heavily discounted.

# Home

I loved the apartment from the moment I first walked in, being a fine example of the kind of architecture I admire most. It was modernist and minimalist yet retained the features and qualities of the building's industrial heritage: a four-metre-high ceiling, elegant steel roof trusses and huge glass-block windows running full-length down one side, flooding the main space with natural light. The unit shown below is almost identical to mine, which was at the top right-hand corner of the street façade. The interior images are of the living area and sleeping platform.

Architect Paul Fairweather had made best possible use of the available space and inherited qualities of the building. The unit's interior design was clever and innovative comprising a raised sleeping platform with storage underneath that was within the main space but distinctly separate from the kitchen/living area. Plus, there were separate bathroom, laundry, and office spaces.

## Home

Basement parking and a shared courtyard with pool, spa, sauna, and barbecue area, completed the package.

My recovery from divorce and burn-out at work was thanks in no small measure to the qualities of 15/27 Ballow Street along with the social life that the common facilities fostered amongst the residents. I quickly made excellent close friends of two lively young couples on the same floor as me. Over the next few years, we were constantly in and out of each other's apartments, enjoying impromptu dinner parties and hanging out by the pool. I frequented the cafes, music venues and art galleries within a short stroll of home, enjoying the kind of urban life that I had last experienced in London, 30 years earlier. As a long-time art lover, I started collecting affordable pieces by young and emerging artists. This was prompted in good part by the four-metre-high, 12-metre-long wall running full length along one side of the unit that was brightly lit by the glass-block windows opposite. It was perfect for mounting a modest art collection that became, and still is, a source of great solace, joy, and inspiration, to me.

In summary, the deeper meaning of that particular home, which I occupied for about five years, is profound. I arrived there in the midst of an emotional crisis and was healed in good part due to the inherent qualities of the unit, the housing complex, and the surrounding urban environment. They provided the context for my new lifestyle and the new relationships that I formed there.

# Home

I moved on from the Valley because I took a year-long contract on the Gold Coast to co-author a sustainable building code for the Currumbin Ecovillage. On the Coast, I rented an apartment right on the beach at Tugun. There was not even a road to cross to get to the wide golden sands of the surf beach. As a long-time surfer and nature lover, I absolutely adored the location. But by the end of that year on the Coast, I was over living alone; I pined to return to community. So after a process of reconnaissance and selection, I moved to the Findhorn spiritual community and ecovillage in North Scotland.

I had been living in Findhorn for about six months when the opportunity came up to design and build another house. By that time, I was working as an architect and project manager for the Findhorn Foundation (FF). I had also fallen in love again, with Barbara, an *Italiana* who remains my closest and most enduring friend although our partnership, as such, lasted only seven years. With loads of architectural nous and a strong sense of the practical, Barbara was invaluable support on the project.

The Foundation wanted to experiment with a new building type that we called an 'ecomobile' – a low-carbon home built in-situ to the regulations governing caravans and mobile homes.* I was

---

\* This boils down to two things:
1) the building requires an above-ground chassis that enables it to be moved (either towed or lifted by crane) and,
2) it can be no more than 18m long and 6m wide.

# Home

briefed to design and construct a small, one-bedroom, mobile home, appropriately designed for a coworker couple (or single) of the FF. I conceived of the house as a retreat – a place of psychological and spiritual nurture. For Foundation coworkers, work life can be very busy, often intense. Every day they interact closely with guests, most of whom they meet as strangers, which can be fun and extremely rewarding, but it is also wearisome, especially for introverts like me. It requires (for me, anyway) that I have a home to return to in the evening where I can recharge my batteries. The other key design driver was climate; I had to get my head around designing for a radically different climate to the subtropical conditions that had governed my design thinking back in Australia. In Scotland, the primary need is protection from cold winters, as opposed to alleviating hot summers. With Barbara's support, I worked extremely hard on the build, mostly single-handed for eight months through the middle of winter, although help from coworkers was always at hand when needed (see below). I was 57 by then, no longer the indestructible young buck of my 20s; I was a physical wreck by the end it.

## Home

At no point during the build could Barbara and I hold any expectation of being able to live in the house. In that sense, our work was a selfless act of service, or 'love in action' as we say. In the Foundation, decisions are made about who will move into vacant accommodation at the time it becomes available. At that point, interested coworkers meet for an attunement, during which the decision is made, mostly based on spiritual guidance received during meditation. The outcome can sometimes seem counter-intuitive, or perhaps even unjust; an attunement is not necessarily predicated on natural justice. But, as things turned out, she and I prevailed in the attunement and were able to move in. We happily lived there together for several years before she went off to Aberdeen to study. I would remain in the house for a total of 12 years until last year (2019) when I retired and left the Foundation.

The building is named Eucalyptus because I came from Australia and there happened to be such a tree growing right next to it. It is located in an area of high ecological value and sensitivity where numerous full-grown specimen trees form a nature corridor linking two areas of wildlife habitat. Because it 'touches the ground lightly,'* resting as it does on just a few pad footings and has a small footprint (physical as well as ecological), such a building can be set amongst the trees with minimal impact. There are several more ecomobiles in the area.

---

* A term popularised by Australian architect, Glenn Murcutt.

# Home

The entrance is approached across a low wooden bridge and under a pergola that carries climbing roses in summer. A conservatory cum entry porch constructed of recycled doors and windows clad in translucent polycarbonate provides a space to gently transition and to deposit coats and shoes. It is lit at night with colour-changing LEDs that offer a light show to passers-by in the street. The progression from street to interior via the bridge (a metaphor for passing from one world to another) is designed as a series of experiences that encourage a subtle energy and mood shift from that of busy work and community life to a more relaxed and tranquil state of being. The building comprises a single main living space, a separate bedroom, and a link between them incorporating bathroom and storage.

# Home

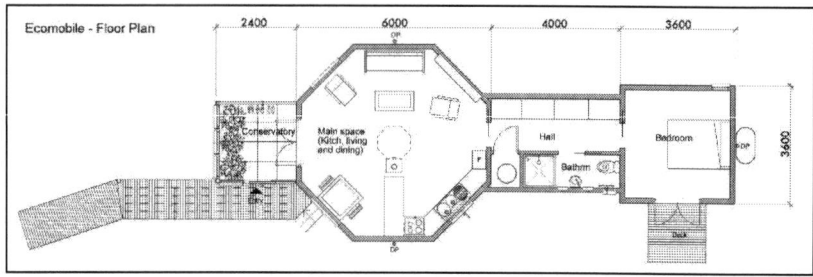

The main space has an octagonal floor plan. Its form and minimalist detailing, free from visual clutter, are intended to induce a feeling of ease and calm. The 135-degree corners are softer and easier on the eye than conventional 90-degree ones. Within the space, separate kitchen, dining and living areas pinwheel about a centrally located wood stove, symbolic of a primeval hearth or fire pit. Each area borrows space and amenity from the others, enabling a much smaller combined footprint.

Large windows and a central skylight deliver high levels of natural light and different views of the surrounding vegetation. The linking corridor (below top left) is similarly flooded with daylight entering through its translucent roof and ceiling. With full-length storage along one side, it doubles as a dressing room. A small but well-appointed bathroom (below top right) with a similar translucent ceiling, incorporates toilet, basin, and shower.

Because clothes are stored elsewhere, the bedroom is minimally furnished with just a bed. Its pure cubic volume (3.3m wide x 3.3m long, x 3.3m high) and minimalist décor induce, to my mind, the qualities of a sacred space or temple. A full-width south-facing clerestory window lets in sun and light and invites views of the stars and full moon. A narrow full-height window to the west offers views of the adjacent pine forest and several ventilation options in summer. An open deck outside the bedroom incorporates a hammock and *ofuro,* a Japanese style soaking bath made from a whisky barrel.

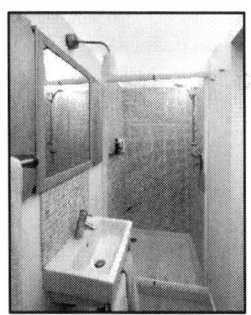

Eucalyptus cost approximately £40,000 to build, which is about half that (per m$^2$) of regular architect-designed and detailed homes in the region. The biggest cost saving was achieved through self-building; the labour component was about 20% of the cost, considerably less than normal. My being both designer and builder reduced the documentation required and eliminated the need for conventional architectural supervision. No planning application or building warrant were required either, because the building was technically a caravan and so, outwith the remit of the Council. Yes!!! Further savings were made through online shopping for materials, fixtures, and fittings (expertly done by Barbara), resulting in many fewer trips to local service centres, which saved time, money, and carbon emissions.

The building is, in truth, poorly oriented for passive solar gain. Site constraints dictated that it be elongated North-South, counter to passive solar design principles. However, the south-facing conservatory and large openings on southern elevations allow considerable solar gain. And anyway, the building receives no direct sunlight in winter, due to the surrounding trees. Heat is mostly provided by a wood stove burning firewood from our own forest whilst there are backup electric wall radiators if required. The boiler is electric. The cooktop is a low-energy induction hob. There is no television, dishwasher, microwave, washing machine or clothes dryer.[*] Because the electricity is generated by our own windmills, the building creates no carbon emissions in its day-to-day operation, so in that sense, can be considered 'zero-carbon.' Furthermore, it probably has the lowest running costs of any building in the ecovillage.

---

[*] I deliberately did not include laundry facilities, preferring to carry my washing to the communal FF laundry once a fortnight in order not have to endure the noise, vibration, and high energy of a washing machine.

# Home

To summarise, Eucalyptus is a vehicle for sustainable living. Designed for a couple or single person, it offers high levels of comfort and amenity whilst enabling the occupants to minimise their environmental footprint. The building is about half the size (per person) of the average British home. Small dwellings require fewer materials to construct, less energy to heat, and can store less accumulated 'stuff.' Beyond material considerations, Eucalyptus provides a supportive setting for *voluntary simplicity* – a less consumerist, more conscious, environmentally benign lifestyle characterised by ease, grace, and beauty. It is an incubator for a contemplative life – a place where the soul may find peace.

On a more personal level, the deeper meaning of my stint in Eucalyptus was similar to, but different from, that of my other homes. Having designed and built it, the fabric of the building felt like a favourite old woollen overcoat. And given the Scottish climate that meant a *lot*. The house was cosy, comfortable, and well lit. Often in winter, with a flickering fire in the place where many would have a TV, with soothing jazz or classical playing over the JBL, a glass of red wine in hand and good company, I was in heaven. So a large part of its value was also to my relationships. In the beginning, it was a container for deepening love with another, and in later years when I lived there alone, it worked just as well as a setting for deepening my relationship with self.

## Home

I came to Findhorn in search of a socially satisfying, ecologically benign, communal life; not to take a spiritual journey as such. So my personal growth and transformation here have been all the more striking for that. Living in Findhorn for 15 years, and in Eucalyptus for 12 of them, has softened both me and my worldview a *lot*! It took its time, but eventually, the spiritual fundamentals of the place worked their magic. As a nurturing container for a process of transformation, Eucalyptus was key.

A recent pic taken by professional photographer, Mark Richards

And finally, to my current dwelling, which as you will see, has been equally important to my journey of personal development. I am now living not far from Eucalyptus at number 442 in the ironically named, Field of Dreams. In the 1990s, enterprising members of the community formed a company to develop much-needed housing in the Park. Housing affordability has always been a major challenge for the community as there has never been enough to meet the demand. They bought the Field (for short) from an adjacent farm and subdivided it along conventional lines, laying in the roads and infrastructure, then selling off serviced plots to individuals and families, on which to build their (dream) houses. Purchasers were required to comply with stringent sustainable building guidelines in the hope that the project would become a model for ecovillage development elsewhere. I think this has largely come to pass. I know for a fact that the Currumbin Ecovillage developers with whom I worked in Australia, had visited Findhorn, and were greatly inspired by the project. In that sense, the developers and the community thought of it, and the Park as a whole, as a 'Planetary Village.'

The developers provided a proportion of affordable housing – a UK-wide requirement of any large new housing project. Their response was to build a row of attached two-storey townhouses, named Centinis after the Italian investor who put up much of the capital. Below is a drone's-eye view of part of the ecovillage. The Field of Dreams occupies the entire foreground of the shot and includes all the homes except for the L-shaped straw-bale house and row of five similar bungalows in the middle distance.

# Home

The row of Centinis is located in the middle, surrounded by larger, privately owned family houses. The house that I occupy is outlined. The arrow at the top indicates the location, behind those trees, of Eucalyptus. Beyond the forest of pines is a mass of wild gorse in full bloom (so this shot must have been taken in May), and beyond that, the Moray Firth, a vast inlet of the North Sea. Beyond that again, on the other side of the Firth, are the northernmost Highlands. In the distance over to the left is the traditional (400 years old) fishing village of Findhorn. It is as young as that (many such villages are centuries older) because originally, it was further to the north (where now there is ocean) but was destroyed during a 17$^{th}$-century storm and rebuilt further back on higher ground. What you cannot see in the photograph, is Findhorn Bay, out of shot to the left, a large tidal estuary that is home to copious wildlife including several species of migrating geese. In the Firth, it is commonplace to see seals, dolphins, porpoise and occasionally otters, orcas, and basking sharks. So there you have it – my wonderful surroundings.

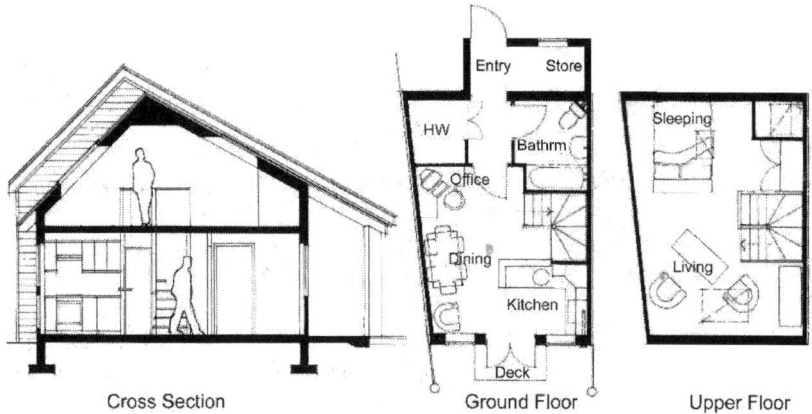

The 14 Centinis are a mix of one- and two-bedroom units, mine being a one-bedder (shown above in section and plan). At 50 m², it is even smaller than Eucalyptus. And, as much as I loved living there, I think I enjoy this place even more. There is one principal reason for that – the sun! As mentioned, Eucalyptus received no direct sunshine for about four months of the year. Its orientation was not ideal for solar gain and it was deliberately designed as a retreat from the world, so, for better or worse, there was no direct access between the living room and the exterior. (Instead, I brought the garden into the porch in the form of large tubs of plants.)

My current home, on the other hand, has full and open exposure to the south, unimpeded by trees, so it gets blasted by the sun all year round. In our climate, that is a huge blessing, even in summer when overheating is seldom a problem. Furthermore, French doors open out from the ground floor onto a deck and the garden. Access and visual connection between the kitchen/dining area and the garden are to die for.

The configuration of spaces is unusual; combining sleeping and living areas is not to everyone's taste. Indeed, many residents of similar units squeeze all their living areas into the ground floor and reserve upstairs entirely for sleeping (I guess to keep it more private). But the way I have it makes much better use of the available space and works well for my lifestyle. I am currently spending 90% of my time upstairs, whilst I write this book. It is warmer up there, of course, and extremely quiet and private, with the same quality of cave-like nurture that I loved so much about Eucalyptus. The sleeping and living areas are subtly separated by a furniture piece I made that combines bedhead, bedside table (with built-in power outlets) and bookshelf. I built it to solve the problem of the restrictive upstairs head height. The way I have the bed positioned is the only option I could devise that allows access to both sides of the bed whilst also avoiding excessive head-bumping. As you can tell from the cross-section, the ceiling is way too low; it should have been at least half a metre higher – one of the few design miscalculations made by the architect, I believe. Here are sufficient pics to illustrate all the different areas: the stairwell and upper-level spaces are shown in the top images; ground floor spaces below that.

# Home

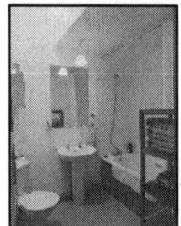

I am a minimalist (as you may be able to tell from the pics); and therein lies a tale. I have always been tidy and organised (to the point of being borderline OCD). Over time, I think my aversion to mess and clutter has become more extreme. And I have become more conscious of the environmental consequences of consumerism. So in the process, I have continuously downsized – slowly shedding accumulated *stuff*. In moving here from Eucalyptus, I took the opportunity to dispense of yet more superfluous possessions. We are fortunate to have an on-site recycling centre, the Boutique, where folk can leave things that they no longer want, for others to take. So into the Boutique went almost everything I had in cupboards that never saw the light of day plus 90% of my books and all my CDs (after I had digitised them to computer and phone). The only belongings I cannot imagine ever shedding are my art pieces. I have had them now for about 20 years and still derive pleasure from seeing them every single day. I am also quite attached to the coffee table, which I made about 25 years ago in the workshop at QUT.

So I have the place just as I like now, which is just as well given that we have been 'locked down' for the last four months under Covid regulations. For me that has been a profound experience, challenging at first but ultimately, richly rewarding. We are, in Findhorn a very huggy community; long, lingering hugs between friends are normative (as they are, in my experience, everywhere that open-hearted people live in community). So adjusting to social isolation took a good couple of months. But at that point, I reached a state of acceptance and surrender, which unexpectedly led me into a deep process of reflection and self-realisation. I had 'space' free from busyness and relationships, enabling me to face my shadow and take a long, hard look at some unhealthy behavioural patterns that I have carried my whole life. And, in coming through that, arrive at a place of deep inner peace – a kind of monastic state of mind and way of being. Everyday domestic life became simple and repetitive, like a Taizé song or mantra. And it has been that way ever since. So my current home, despite not having been designed and built by me, has become as deeply meaningful to me as any other. I am feeling incredibly grateful as I finish this chapter, for this and all the other dwellings in which I have lived.

# Home

Image by photojournalist, Ed Gold.

# Journeys

I have always loved travelling. The reasons are numerous, but I think it is my passion for research and learning, particularly about history, culture, and place, that excites me. Actually, it is the synthesis of these three things that I find most fascinating, i.e., how humans adapt their environment over time in culturally distinct ways. Over the years, I have made many journeys to ancient and historic sites, and where possible, sought immersive cultural experiences. I have taken very few holidays purely for pleasure or relaxation. I just would not know how to relax beside a pool with a drink and a view; I am way too driven to get out, explore and discover.

## MY MOST MEMORABLE JOURNEY

Wonderful in its own right, a journey that I took in 1972 was particularly compelling because I was an impressionable 21-

year-old, and this was my first foray beyond the shores of New Zealand and Australia to the unknown world beyond. It was my earliest experience of diverse cultures, exotic languages, and historic places. I travelled first to the US with two close Habonim friends, then on to the UK. We were joined in London by two more Habo comrades and the five of us travelled overland to Israel. En route, I fell hopelessly in love with Europe – a love that would draw me back 30 years later to live in Scotland. I have often wondered why I adore Europe quite so much. I felt it as soon as I landed in London and the feeling deepened as we journeyed through Holland, Belgium, France, Switzerland, Germany, Liechtenstein, Italy, and Greece, before terminating the trip in Israel. In a word, I think the attraction is *age*!

The towns and cities of NZ and Australia were barely 100 years old when I was a kid. There were no ancient buildings and hardly any historic ones. I do not recall a single cobbled street. Of course, both countries have rich indigenous cultures stretching back hundreds and thousands of years. But there was little experience of that in my childhood that was not staged for tourists. I recognised the dearth of historical features in NZ as aa small child. 'Where were the castles, palaces and manor houses of my storybooks?' I wondered, and for that matter, 'Where are the exotic costumes and traditional festivals?' However, on arrival in London, I immediately felt like a character in one of those books. The rich street life and tangible evidence of ageing were everywhere. I also felt a strong sense of arriving home! So perhaps my family's roots being deep in the soil of Belarus and Latvia is also a factor in my enduring Europhilia.

We began the trip in Fiji, with me coming from Sydney and my companions from NZ. But before even getting to Europe, we had first to navigate the United States via Honolulu, LA, and NYC. (Long-haul flights were much shorter in those days). Being in transit in Hawaii was bad enough. I had never seen cops routinely carrying guns before. They never have in NZ and did not in Australia at that time. And these were sub-machine guns, which scared the hell out of me. From there, it was on to LA for a meal out with relatives of one of us and then on to Manhattan for a week. My companions had relatives to stay with. All I had was the address of a friend of a friend with whom I could crash. His apartment (if you could call it that) was located on the top floor of a derelict five-storey walk-up on East 13th Street.. It had no hot water and even the cold tap ran at a trickle.

The Lower East Side of Manhattan at the time was an extremely disadvantaged district, socially and economically. The historical views below (not my photographs) typify what I found. The street out front of our building was like a war zone – home (literally) to hookers, junkies, and pushers. I am aware that these terms are extremely pejorative, but the horror I was feeling made it hard to get beyond my biases at the time. I was just too young and naive. On descending five flights of rickety stairs each morning, I would need to climb over sleeping homeless folk in the entrance to get to the front door. Signs of poverty and deprivation were everywhere. Then on the third day, I saw someone attempting suicide by placing their head under the wheel of a bus waiting to leave from a stop. He did not succeed, thank God, but witnessing the attempt freaked me out.

It was the last straw; I just had to get out of there. I contacted one of my companions, whom I knew was staying with cousins. On hearing my story, they kindly invited me out to their place, which happened to be in affluent Great Neck, Long Island. I arrived to discover that the cousins lived in total luxury – at the far end of the socio-economic spectrum to my experience of the previous three days. Although I was extremely grateful, I found this equally troubling. It was my first exposure to the extremes of wealth and poverty that characterise American capitalism and as an avowed Marxist at the time, I was horrified by the disparity.

Once safely in London, we met up with our remaining two friends for a week of wide-eyed tourism. It was June 1972, and the weather was hot. We walked streets of Monopoly fame, drank in beer gardens of traditional pubs, attended the cricket at Lords, visited famous castles, parks and museums and generally, soaked up the history and culture. Then it was on to Amsterdam, where for US$400 we purchased a VW Kombi that eventually (15,000 miles later) we sold for US$400 in Rome. It was a stock standard, no-frills Kombi, but it never missed a beat throughout the whole journey; I do not think we even had a puncture.

Pictured above are the intrepid five with our trusty steed: myself on the roof, then from left to right, Geoff, Tanya, Johnny, and Mike. We travelled with five backpacks, a camp stove, a single large pot, and some utensils. At night we would flatten the bench seats and four of us would sleep like sardines across the back whilst, Geoff, who was two metres tall, would sleep in the front with his feet sticking out the door. We cooked once a day, usually after parking up at night, and the menu was almost always the same – a huge pot of vegetable soup made from fresh produce purchased daily from a town market. We named it People Soup because we distributed the surplus to other young travellers and anyone else who wanted or needed. I fondly recall the time we brazenly fed the homeless in front of the rich and famous at an outdoor restaurant in St Tropez. Yes! Our minor revolutionary act was also a great way to meet other travellers and get tips on places to visit. In the days before smartphones and satellite navigation, we were reliant on folding paper maps and word of mouth to get around. Staying in touch with family involved sending an aerogramme once a week and receiving letters via *Poste Restante*. It was a different era back then and, I think, all the better for it!

We drove down through Belgium where I recall we woke one morning to find that we had inadvertently parked overnight in the middle of a market square. All around us, vendors had set up their stalls, some tying guy ropes to our van's mirrors and door handles. We were ensnared all morning but left fully stocked with freely donated supplies of fresh food. (Belgium has the best hot chips by the way, or at least, the best presented.) I well remember a similar case of inappropriate overnight parking in rural France. We woke to loud knocking on the van's windows and climbed out sleepily to be confronted by a hostile farmer and his four sons, all armed with shotguns. We saw immediately that we had inadvertently parked amongst their precious grapevines. We could not speak French nor they English, but once we had convinced them (with gesticulation) that we meant no harm, they became super friendly and took us back to their farmhouse for breakfast accompanied by a glass or two of their wine.

We visited Paris of course, still one of my fave cities anywhere. We parked up by the Seine on the outskirts of town and indulged in the cultural offerings of that stunning city. But actually, my most abiding memory of that visit is of the baguettes and brie that we had for breakfast, not to mention the quality wine at super low cost. From there we drove down to Avignon, a classical walled mediaeval city where we enjoyed a show in the ruined citadel, amongst other delights. And on we went, to Monaco, the Riviera and into Switzerland where at one point, we met some locals at a lookout, got chatting and were invited back to their place for an authentic Swiss fondue with all the trimmings. It was these kinds of interactions with locals that we valued most, and in the days before mass tourism, there was a great deal of openness toward travellers. Another, less agreeable memory I have of Switzerland, was setting out to cross a street and hearing a screech of brakes followed by the feel of a half-tonne weight on the toe of my boot. I had stepped off the curb whilst looking the wrong way, of course, which was a lesson we probably all learned the hard way at some point. Fortunately, my sturdy hiking boots saved the day.

We had planned all along to arrive in Munich for the beginning of the 1972 Olympic Games. As young Jews, most of whom had lost family during WWII, we knew that visiting Germany was going to be emotionally challenging. However, three of the five of us were avid sports fans and the Olympics proved too hard to resist. Our emotional aversion got overruled by our love of sport. But before arriving in Munich, we visited the concentration camp of Dachau, just to the north. Speaking for myself, this was both horrifying and strangely healing. It unexpectedly (and literally, I suppose) put some ghosts to rest. And it helped me resolve, at least in part, my ambivalence toward Zionism. Not that I have ever had an issue with Jews deserving a permanent home of their own, secure and free from persecution. I just happen to think that Palestinians deserve the same, which they do not yet have.

For the week we were there, the Olympics were a total blast. In a deliberate attempt to wipe the stain of the 1936 fascist games from memory, the IOC and German organisers had tagged them the 'Carefree Games,' deliberately playing up the joy of sporting competition for the athletes and the fun and excitement for spectators. And in keeping with this theme, they had fatefully decided to keep security low key; as far as I could tell, it was almost non-existent. It was a decision that would come back to haunt them. We had tickets, of course, but we also had no difficulty jumping fences to enter some venues, including the main stadium. On one memorable occasion, the day of the 3000m Steeplechase and 100m Sprint finals, I even jumped down into the photographers' pit that ringed the running track and spent the whole day there, despite being politely asked to leave several times. We attended multiple events including gymnastics, table tennis, archery, and rowing (at a time when NZ dominated the sport). At the basketball, I made my way down onto the court during a game between Australia and the US and took photographs from right under the hoop. Looking back, I am amazed that I got away with it. But as mentioned, there was little concern about security, the unspeakable consequences of which would become all too clear within days.

On leaving Munich, two of our band of travellers split to do their own thing and three of us drove down to Northern Italy via the curious principality of Liechtenstein. We headed for Genova where there was a cousin of one of us, with whom we could stay. And it was there that we (and the world) watched in horror for 24 hours whilst events unfolded back in Munich. I mentioned the Munich massacre to a friend recently and she said that she had never heard of it, which surprised me. If anyone reading this is similarly unaware, I would respectfully suggest that you inform yourself; it was one of the key historical events of the 20$^{th}$ century, not least because it transformed security arrangements at large public events forever after. I would recommend the film, *One Day in September*, as a reasonably accurate portrayal of events. In short, eight members of the Palestinian terrorist group, Black September, took nine members of the Israeli Olympic team hostage in their accommodation, having initially killed two more. All nine died during a botched rescue attempt by the German police.

Glued to a TV, we were mortified by the unfolding drama. In retrospect, it was like watching the Twin Towers coming down on 9/11; the horror was similarly overwhelming. We considered abandoning the rest of the journey and heading straight for Israel, we were so shaken, but ultimately decided to continue. So with heavy hearts, we headed south as planned, first to Pisa then Florence and eventually, to Rome. Our time in Italy is a bit of a blur in my mind. We were amused by Pisa's leaning tower, of course. I loved Florence for the way I felt transported back to the Renaissance. And in Rome, I was deeply moved by seeing and touching ruins that stretched back 3000 years. The atmosphere of the city seemed thick with historical significance. We parked up at the Spanish steps, which is where we sold our van.

Decades later, I would revisit all of these places and more in Italy. It remains one of my favourite countries anywhere in the world. In fact, all the countries of Southern Europe are amongst my favourites: Portugal, Spain, Italy, and Greece. I have not been to

## Journeys

Croatia, Cyprus, or Malta, but I imagine they would appeal for similar reasons – the integration of history, culture, and place. And when you throw in the weather and cuisine, what's not to love? Indeed, before Brexit raised its ugly head, I fantasised that I might, one day, live somewhere in Southern Europe.

We next took a train to Brindisi on Italy's east coast and boarded the ferry for Athens. On arrival, we checked into a hostel then made a beeline for the Acropolis. In those days, there were few tourists and almost no restrictions on movement in and around the ruins. We were able to freely feel, touch, smell and soak up the atmosphere of the Parthenon, the Temple of Athena, and the other wonders on that ancient, ancient site. I was awe-struck knowing that this place (amongst others in the city) was the birthplace of Western culture – that our religion, philosophy, politics, laws, economics, customs, and so on, were all conceived right here! At the time, my understanding of architectural history was based on high school history lessons and reading. It would be another 20 years before an architectural education would enable me to fully appreciate the sophistication of the buildings on the Acropolis. And it would be a further 20 before I could return there armed with greater understanding and maturity and be able to more deeply relive the experience, albeit with the additional challenge of $21^{st}$ century crowds and security measures.

## Journeys

We spent just a couple of days in Athens then took a ferry from Piraeus to our final stopover, Poros. To complete the trip, we had allocated a full week of rest and recreation. And what an inspired plan that turned out to be! My first taste of the Greek Islands was one of the most memorable stops of the whole journey. Poros is a small island not far from Athens. Back then it was an overlooked destination for travellers who generally headed for the outer Aegean islands (and still do, I imagine). As far as I could tell, we were the only English speakers on the island. And I do not recall meeting any residents who could speak English.

That did not stop us feeling perfectly at home amongst them, such was the conviviality of the local people. We ate, drank, and laughed with the elders in the tavernas and played football with the kids on dusty improvised pitches. The island was picture-postcard perfect with traditional white flat-roofed houses spilling down the hillside to the waterfront lined with open-air cafés, restaurants, and bars. In those days, such venues were there (and felt like they had always been there) just for the locals, who seemed to dine out every evening. So the prices were ridiculously low, the food was authentic and amazing, as were the wine, the setting, the ambience, and of course, the balmy late summer weather. From Poros, we went back to Athens and directly to the airport, excited in anticipation of reaching our destination, Israel. As with Italy, this taste of the Greek Islands would draw me back decades later. The experience has been quite different of course;

tourism has changed them. But the essentials remain the same: the evocative architecture and landscapes; the warmth and hospitality of the people; the relaxed lifestyle; delicious cuisine; and near-perfect summer weather. Sadly, Greece's national and local economies have become reliant on tourism (and clearly, I have been complicit in that). I can only imagine that the 2020 pandemic has been devastating for all sectors of their economy. It has also ravaged the travel industry generally, with very few people flying at all these days, least of all for a holiday.

## MORE GREAT JOURNEYS

My very first travel adventure (other than family holidays) was for rest and recuperation. It came when I was 12, following the dramatic illness described in the chapter, Childhood. My folks felt that I needed a holiday to aid recovery – psychological rather than physical since I was fully repaired by that time but still somewhat traumatised by the experience. So Dad took me off to Mt Ruapehu for a week of skiing.

## Journeys

We stayed in the famous Chateau Tongariro Hotel, lauded by Tim Roxborogh in the NZ Herald as "New Zealand's most luxurious hotel [complete with] fluoro-blue swimming pool housed in an underground wartime infirmary, location without peer, rumours of hauntings, secret passageways, a cinema, [and] a place the Queen once stayed." The whole scenario seemed impossibly exotic to me.

I enjoyed my first taste of skiing. Even as a learner I fell in love with the sport, probably for much the same reason that I remain enamoured of golf and surfing – it offers an immersive experience of nature in all its awe-inspiring beauty. After a couple of lessons, I was ready to take the lift up to an intermediate level slope. I learned quickly and was soon outpacing Dad on the ski runs, which actually, almost proved disastrous. My most vivid memory of the whole trip was skiing off-piste away from him and having to make an awkward emergency stop to avoid falling into a bottomless abyss! Only then did it sink in, why an entire lesson on the previous day had been devoted to learning how to stop in a hurry.

My second significant trip as a youngster was to Sydney when I was 14. Travelling overseas for the first time, alone, made it memorable enough, but I remember it well for at least two further reasons. I stayed with an old school friend of mum's. She and her husband owned one of a cluster of three famous houses designed by Australia's preeminent modernist architect, Harry Seidler. The home itself was stunning enough but I was actually most taken by the trio of like buildings set as they were amongst native trees and bushland. The experience may well have spawned my love of site planning in architectural design and the idea of a campus of related buildings. There was another, more nefarious reason, that I recall this trip so well. My hostess was a kind and generous woman, to a fault. She let me drive her car unsupervised at the age of 14, which in Australia, was two years underage. I had a certain fascination with cars and speed at the time; not that her Ford A40 was capable of going very fast. But it was quick enough to enable me to hone my cornering skills around the mercifully quiet and traffic-free streets of Wahroonga, one of Sydney's affluent northern suburbs.

Whilst living in Israel in my early 20s, I undertook numerous journeys in space and time. Many of them were historically transporting – back to biblical times, or the Roman occupation, or medieval crusades. Never was history more intriguing to me than on those trips. I was able to contextualise stories from the Old Testament, which finally enabled me to make sense of them. For the first time in my life, I think, I felt fully Jewish.

One particular trip was also pivotal, spiritually. I was on *tiyul* (tour) in the Sinai Desert (pictured above but not by me) with a bus full of 20-somethings. We arrived at the foot of Mt Sinai in the evening and set up camp, planning to climb to the legendary Greek Orthodox monastery, Santa Caterina, in the morning. Late that night, I went for a walk on my own in the desert. After some time, I sat on a rock to rest. In those days I was sceptical and closed-minded – anything but open to transcendental experience. And yet, in that moment something magical, nay mystical, occurred. I can only surmise that what happened was due to the conditions in which I found myself: being in the middle of a vast, vast desert; one that is completely arid and devoid of vegetation; where the air is as dry and clean as anywhere on Earth; on a night when the stars were as bright and as numerous as I had ever seen in my life. Due to the context and rarefied atmosphere, I was somehow able to soften my defences, let down my guard, and allow myself an experience of the infinite – of 'oneness.'

As I sat on the rock, I slowly became aware of my connection with it – the rock and I were made of the same fundamental stuff, stardust, and we were, in fact, one. My attention was then drawn to the sand around the rock and I 'saw' the same elemental interconnection between the rock on which I sat and the sand upon which it rested. So now I am one with both the rock and the desert floor; we form a continuum at a sub-atomic level. Soon my awareness expanded further out to include the surrounding *wadi* (valley), so I now felt interconnected and as one with everything up to and including the mountains all around. Slowly, iteratively, my awareness expanded onward and outward to include the whole desert, the region, the Earth, the stars and, ultimately, the whole damned Universe. I felt at one with all that is. I do not know how long the experience lasted, perhaps five or ten minutes, or perhaps one or two; I really have no idea. But when I came to, I was left with the unshakeable conviction that I, we, everything, is fully interconnected. From that day onward I have taken this to be an incontrovertible truth because, it seems, I had it proven to me! I 'saw' it with my own eyes. Did I literally see it? I do not know. Perhaps our inner visual faculties are capable of such things. But the whys and wherefores are irrelevant – by some means or other, I arrived at a crystal clear understanding of an essential truth that has lived in me ever since.

During my time as an architectural lecturer, I worked hard to provide my students with opportunities to broaden their understanding of cultures other than their own, which for most was middle-class, white Australian, i.e., bland, material, and provincial, if not bigoted. Field trips are the best vehicle for achieving this, so I tried to organise at least one with each cohort of second- or third-year students, usually combined with a design project for, and with, a community group as client. The most ambitious of these adventures was to Indonesia. I took 30 students and two close colleagues in support. We spent a week in each of three very different locations: Jakarta, Jogjakarta, and Bali. In the capital, we stayed on campus at the University of Indonesia and worked collaboratively with students there. It was back in the days before stringent risk assessment of field trips, which is just as well because there is no way I could possibly have anticipated the high jinks the students would get up to.

My supervision policy was always to treat the students (who were mostly aged 20) as the adults they were and to trust their judgement. Ha, ha!! Here are just two stories that made their way back to me. Apparently, a few of them befriended members of the local mafia, probably at the night markets surrounding the campus. They rode with them, so the story goes, on the backs of motorbikes at high speed through the streets of Jakarta, some said on drug runs. On another occasion, they collaborated with local students in squeezing 27 individuals into and on top of a jeep before careering around the campus at two in the morning.

We next went to Jogja in central Java because it is one of the centres of traditional Javanese culture, particularly architecture, batik, drama, and puppetry. There, the students were required to compile a daily journal of sketches, observations, and reflections. Looking back, it was fortunate that in 1997 they were without the distraction of smartphones and social media, which enabled them to more fully immerse in the rich cultural offerings of the place. One morning at 5:00, we bussed to nearby Borobudur (below), the world's largest Buddhist archaeological ruin, a pyramid of sorts. Getting there early enabled us to avoid both the tourists and the heat. For many, it was the first time that they had encountered any sort of ancient ruin up close and I could tell they were deeply moved by the experience.

From Jogja we flew to Bali for a week without structure or programme; the students were free to do whatever they wished. Some went surfing whilst others hired scooters and toured the island. Fortunately, they all repaid my trust by returning to base (Ubud) in one piece. The week also enabled us three staff to relax and explore. Bali is principally Hindu, so our time there visiting numerous temples and participating in rituals and festivals, complimented our experience of Islam in Jakarta and Buddhism in Jogja. (Indonesia has five official religions.) For youngsters who had mostly never left Australia, it was an invaluable taste of cultures other than their own. I still get emails, 25 years on, from some of those students for whom the trip, they say, was the highlight of their architectural studies.

In 2000, my final year as an academic, I travelled to Durban as part of an exchange between QUT and the University of Natal. I was picked up from the airport and taken directly to an outdoor music festival. My host, Kevin, and I walked into the site to join a seething, mixed-race crowd picnicking together in convivial harmony. I made my way up to the front (since I was a keen gig photographer in those days) just as my long-time jazz idol, Hugh Masakela, walked on stage. What a treat that was, and it set the tone for the remainder of my visit.

Durban as a city invites comparison with my then hometown of Brisbane, topographically and climatically. They are on the same latitude and both are on the east coast of a huge landmass, so they have a near-identical climate. And both are within easy reach of beautiful beaches and a sub-tropical hinterland. But there, the similarities end. Culturally, they could not be more different.

Brisbane does have a lively contemporary art, drama, and music scene, but you have to dig for it under the surface. In Durban, it is totally in your face. The culture there is at its richest on the streets and in the outdoor markets. Food, music, fashion, art, craft, and music all intermingle with a vibrancy that is true of the Rainbow Nation, generally, but in Durban is enhanced by the indigenous traditions and culture of the irrepressible Zulu people.

I was there for six weeks of teaching in a third year studio in which the students were roughly a third black, a third white and a third of Indian heritage. Socially, these groups did not mix much although they collaborated well enough on projects. I got to know them all sufficiently well to be invited to their separate parties. The black parties were by far the liveliest – wild, even – the Indian ones, the most sumptuous, and the white ones, the most alcohol-fuelled. All were tremendous fun. Recreation was a big part of their lives, it seemed. The students there lived much more in the moment than mine back in Brisbane. As apartheid had ended just a few years earlier, I guess they were still getting their rocks off!

At one point, I travelled from Durban north to Swaziland and then on to Mozambique. Swazi, now named Eswatini, is a lush gorgeous looking country – high in the mountains yet with a sub-tropical climate. It is one of the few in Africa to have largely escaped the ravages of European colonialism, not least due to its stable, if not patriarchal and anachronistic, absolute monarchy. Not so with Mozambique, however, which suffered 400 years of Portuguese occupation followed, relatively recently, by 15 years of vicious civil war, the scars of which are all too visible to the casual visitor. And whilst it is a reasonably stable republic now, Mozambique remains one of the poorest countries on Earth. Since my travelling in Africa has been limited to this way-too-short sojourn in its southwest, I am to this day very grateful for the experience. I would love to return to this spectacular and hugely diverse continent but doubt that it will ever happen.

By contrast, over the last 25 years, I have done a *lot* of travelling in North America, Asia, and Europe. Some of these trips, taken as part of the doctoral fieldwork and/or communal studies, I mentioned in the last chapter. Others were taken recreationally, mostly in Europe. And whilst north Scotland is somewhat remote, it is still within easy reach of the Continent by train, ferry, or air travel.

Journeys

Probably my most memorable European sojourn was made by Eurail with Barbara, my partner at the time. We set out from home by train for Newcastle where we boarded an overnight ferry to Amsterdam, forever one of my favourite European capitals. After several delightful days there, we picked up the first leg of our Eurail journey all the way across to Budapest, Hungary, where we stayed at the Gellért, a historic Art Nouveau hotel and spa (illustrated below) on the banks of the lazy Danube River. Barbara had stayed there once before and was keen to go back. It was my first taste of such design opulence and I loved it.

As an architectural designer, I tend to take a modernist (i.e., rationalist and minimalist) approach. And yet, I also have a deep love and appreciation of more flamboyant, expressive styles such as Art Nouveau. This trip would prove to be an architectural 'grand tour' of such delights including works by Friedensreich Hundertwasser and the Secessionists in Vienna; Rudolf Steiner, Zaha Hadid, Tadao Ando, Frank Gehry, and others in Basel; Antoni Gaudi in Barcelona; and Gehry again in northern Spain. Since my design education in Australia included no first-hand experience of the work of these icons, this trip was like an architectural erotic dream. Recommended highlights include: the historic landmarks and buildings of Budapest including the 400-year-old synagogue, the largest in Europe; Hundertwasser Haus and a museum dedicated to his art in Vienna; and in Basel, the built legacy of Rudolf Steiner and the Vitra collection of architectural follies. All of these cities straddle beautiful rivers and offer endless opportunities for promenading and/or indulging in the cafes and bars along their banks.

But the absolute standout highlight of the trip for me as an architect was my first visit to Barcelona and the buildings of Antoni Gaudi. I was overwhelmed with emotion in several, such is their power and beauty. The Sagrada Familia is, of course, a tour de force; one of Europe's most visited tourist attractions for good reason. Its sheer beauty, the ambition of Gaudi's vision, the references to nature throughout, and the total integration of all these aspects, is pure genius! Above is a view of the ceiling that I shot lying on my back in the centre of the nave, for which they almost threw me out!

Gaudi's two apartment buildings, Casa Batlló and Casa Milà, are no less wonderful, to my mind. Their glorious atria are pictured below. Although partially occupied (I think), they are very accessible to the public. They possess many of the same attributes as the cathedral (beauty, natural references, and design integration) but in addition, have the intimacy and domestic scale of residential buildings. I feel it would be a disservice to attempt to describe them any further. I'll simply say, "Go visit! Just go!" (But not in mid-summer when crowds can kill the experience.)

Barbara and I were joined in Barcelona by my daughter, Anna. We rented a car and took off across Catalonia and the Basque region, stopping in Pamplona and the Rioja wine area, en route to Bilbao. We visited a winery designed by Frank Gehry (below left) that I thought was pure facadism, but I found the Bilbao Guggenheim much more convincing. The atrium (below right) is truly spectacular.

 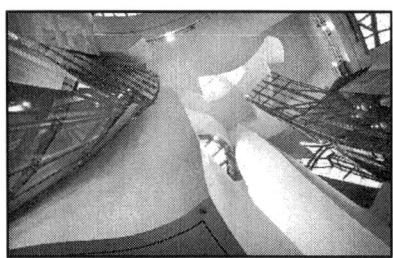

I realise that my account of this trip reads as if it was organised around my personal (architectural) interests, and not those of my companion(s). But in fact, we did much more than just visit buildings. We walked countless streets of cultural and historical interest, visited numerous museums and galleries, attended gigs, concerts and festivals, and enjoyed many fine meals in cafes and restaurants. One memorable cultural highlight came near the end of the trip when we happened upon an annual *paella* festival right near our accommodation in Bilbao. Social groupings of eight or more friends, who mostly had been participating every year since high school, gathered onsite the night before the main event to set up camp and reconnect. Then all through the next day each encampment prepared and cooked over open fires, huge metre-wide platters of their favourite paella. The stories, laughter, and alcohol, all flowed liberally in true Basque style. Late in the afternoon, the platters were paraded ceremonially to a large arena and following tasting and judging, the winners were declared and celebrated. The day ended with participants and spectators, alike, digging in to an amazing variety of sumptuous offerings.

En route to our penultimate destination, San Sebastian, we happened across another festival of sorts in Gipuzkoa, a harbour town on the coast. All along the massive concrete harbour walls, groups of mostly young people were gathered, seemingly for the sole purpose of getting extremely drunk together (as evidenced below). In the process, many fell, jumped, or were pushed into the sea, several meters below. I feared for their safety but perhaps that just signifies the difference between my conservative (Kiwi) cultural background and theirs (Basque).

Journeys

We read that San Sebastian was reputed to have the best *pinchos* (traditional Basque tapas) so we spent our last evening happily testing the theory, enjoying a progressive meal as we strolled from one café to the next, along ancient narrow lanes. So yet again, a rich blend of place, history, cuisine, and culture had provided a fitting end to our time in Spain. From there, Barbara and I boarded a train for Bordeaux from where we flew home, but not before we enjoyed an evening drink in the most elegant wine bar I have ever entered.

And so ended a truly magical European journey, crisscrossing the continent I love so much. Over the years, Barbara and I have taken many more European journeys together including two to her native country, Italy, visiting cities of Renaissance fame (Venice, Verona, Mantua, Siena, and Florence (pictured below)) and others equally alluring but less well known, so less crowded with tourists.

We have also taken two holidays in the Greek Islands (on Santorini and Rhodes), one in Paris, and another in Tenerife. And it was a particular joy to be able to show her and her mother around Israel in 2010, not least because her mum is a devout Catholic so, for her, visiting the Christian religious sites in Jerusalem and elsewhere was a true pilgrimage.

So clearly, over the last 15 years, I have made good use of the proximity of Scotland to the Continent, which was a motivation (albeit a secondary one) for moving here in the first place. And for that, I am deeply grateful. I have gained a much greater appreciation of my cultural roots and our shared human history. It has deepened my understanding of what got me here and, therefore, my sense of self. And from that has flowed immense gratitude, to all the people who have supported me and for the gift of life itself. I wish for my grandchildren that they have opportunities to travel as widely. I wish that it similarly supports them to discover their roots, find themselves, and so develop their true potential.

SCOTTISH JOURNEYS

After completing the last section, I was left asking myself, "But what about Scotland?" So here we are – journeys I have taken to quintessential Sottish locations, all marked on the map below: rural (the famous Highlands), urban (my favourite cities), and coastal (unique spots all around the coastline). But first, a bit of a rave and a declaration of love for this country I have called home for the last 15 years. I have permanent residency in the UK and, for the first time ever, am registered to vote, having previously been a conscientious objector to party politics and not even registered in Australia where it is compulsory. My original motivation was so that I could vote for Scottish independence.

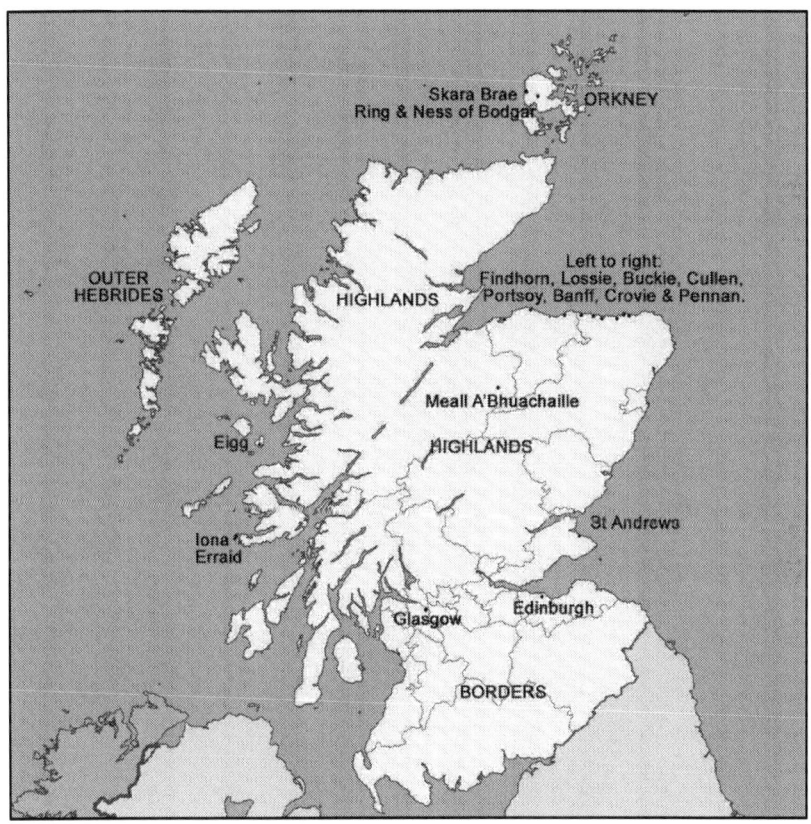

On hearing that I grew up in New Zealand and then spent 30 years in Australia, people often ask why I choose to live in Scotland when I could be living there – the implication being that Australia has much more to offer. I imagine that they're thinking something like: Australia = warm weather, Scotland = cold;

# Journeys

Australia = new world, Scotland = old country; Australia = land of opportunity, Scotland = dead end, etc. The question is both easy to answer and tough to rationalise. The easy answer is, I am here because I have chosen to live in the Findhorn community, of which there is no equivalent in Australia. The difficulty I have in so doing (and my greatest challenge), is something they have not usually considered. My family lives down under: my ageing mum whose health is not the best; my two daughters whom I love with all my being (one in Oz and the other now in NZ); four grandchildren whom I am watching grow up via the Internet; and three siblings. To be living in Scotland, about as far from them as it is possible to get, is hugely conflicting. I have dealt with it by travelling to see them as often as possible (every one or two years) and making regular phone and Skype calls. But it is tough!

The Findhorn community is international, and in that sense, it could be situated anywhere. The demographic profile of residents and guests gives no indication of it being located in Scotland. And yet to me, its context is highly relevant. I cannot imagine living in any intentional community where I felt disconnected or alienated from the surrounding environs and culture. Fortunately, the opposite is true; I love almost everything about this country: its culture, history, and politics. I enjoy partaking of two national treasures, golf, and whisky, and adore the stunning landscapes. I can even handle the climate and I enjoy the seasonality that it brings. I struggled with the summer weather in Brisbane much more than I do the Scottish winters; one can at least dress appropriately for cold weather. And I do not at all value the colonial history, culture, and especially the politics of Australia. I find most of it alienating.

It is the extraordinary landscapes here, in particular, that touch me most – they are so pristine and undeveloped. Scotland is under-populated, particularly in the North, where there is little or no ongoing visible change to either rural or urban environments. The countryside appears to be almost free from development. For better or worse, even new houses here look like old ones! There is little traffic and the mountainscapes are exquisitely beautiful. Some people find them alienating due to the scarcity of trees. But I find them stunning! Let's see if I can illustrate that with a story.

I once set out with four friends to spend a late summer's day hiking in the mountains. We drove about an hour from Findhorn to a town called Aviemore, a famous Highland destination for hikers, skiers, and nature lovers. We drove on another 15 minutes, to the base of Mount Cairngorm, Scotland's most well-known winter skiing destination. In summer, the area is popular for its flora, fauna, water sports, and hiking opportunities. We planned to climb, not Cairngorm itself (4080 ft), but the much less challenging Meall A'Bhuachaille (2650 ft) which, to be honest, is just a foothill. But it is perfect for a relatively easy mountain walking experience through diverse landscapes and ecosystems. The whole area is a National Park, indeed Britain's largest,* yet is mostly privately owned (some would say, "was stolen") by the English aristocracy, and in this particular case, the Queen herself.

We set out on foot from the car park, heading uphill through plantation pine forest and also areas that had been clear-felled, where the vegetation was struggling to re-establish. Some of our group expressed sadness at seeing little regrowth since their last visit two years earlier. Once we got above the tree line the landscape changed radically and the views opened up. At that time of year, the heather is in full bloom. So for the next hour, we walked through a lush lavender coloured carpet of heather up a recently constructed path-cum-stairway of local stone (pictured

---

* Cairngorms National Park covering 4,528 square km was established in 2003 under the National Parks (Scotland) Act 2000.

above). Further up the mountain, we met the National Parks volunteers who were valiantly extending the route.

As we came closer to the top, the heather gave way to a barren, rocky moonscape (of shale, mostly) and the wind started to howl. It amazed me how we had no consciousness of the wind until we neared the summit and then, suddenly, without any apparent change in the weather, it became a gale. Easy to see how ill-prepared or inexperienced and sometimes even expert hikers regularly get caught out and perish in these mountains. I was glad I had borrowed good quality outdoor gear from a work colleague. It was very cold, although not quite the minus seven degrees (with wind chill) that I had seen forecast.

At the top, we sheltered in a ruined stone bothy (wee hut) with several other hikers, all wearing brightly coloured mountain gear. We pulled out our packed lunches of sandwiches, fruit, nuts, chocolate, and thermoses of tea. High on the experience, we ate in reverent silence. It was a bit like a ritual of the initiates, and I felt honoured to be there. Visibility was good and the 360-degree views were stunning. We could see countless other mountains, hills, and valleys, and about a dozen blue and green lochs scattered all about, with hardly a road or a building as far as the eye could see. Wet weather surrounded us, which we enjoyed watching move rapidly across the landscape. But some was heading our way, so after eating, we posed for the obligatory group selfie and headed back down, but by a different route.

We descended on the other side of the mountain with the wind at our backs. I was grateful for the walking poles I had borrowed. It felt like they were all that stood between staying on my feet and being blown all the way down the slope. Once down a hundred feet or so, the wind died as quickly as it had sprung up on the ascent. Way down below, we could see tiny Lochan Uaine, our next stop. We paused briefly at an intact bothy (mountain hut), a facility provided free by National Parks for hikers and skiers, in which to take shelter or perhaps sleep overnight. The interior was minimalist in the extreme with just a fireplace and a built-in wooden window seat. I could live in it, I thought!

We stopped at Lochan Uaine, a mysterious phenomenon, actually, being one of those rare lochs without a watercourse running in or out. There was an eerie green colour to the water and what seemed like submerged ramparts, which turned out to be huge, bleached logs. We investigated an area of woods with a dense undergrowth of ferns and brackens. A path led to a recently constructed platform and seat overlooking the loch – the perfect place for an impromptu ceilidh. A member of our group showed himself to be an excellent tin whistle player. The rest of us danced as light rain began to fall. It was a sweet moment.

Journeys

We pressed on as bad weather was threatening. We chose a return route through what is called the Caledonian Reserve (pictured above) – remnant old-growth forest containing ancient native Scots pines (500+ years old) and a diversity of other trees, including juniper, birch, willow, rowan, and aspen. These are powerful awe-inspiring places, dense with vegetation and wildlife. We walked in single file and awestruck silence but for the accompaniment of the tin whistle, up and down along a narrow pathway that passed close by some incredibly gnarled old trees. The thick vegetation was wet and pungent. The whole thing felt to me like a clip from Lord of the Rings. I think it took me back to childhood and hiking in dense New Zealand rainforest. I loved it! We got back to the car all too soon and headed for home. The atmosphere in the car was one of deep contentment – tired bodies and engaged hearts, high on nature and nourished by the company.

There was a period in which my partner, Barbara, was studying in the ancient seaside town of St Andrews, so I got to know the place well. St Andrews is famous for at least two things – its ancient university and as the 'home' of golf. So for a life-long golfer and once academic, the place has tremendous appeal. It is a compact city, very walkable, and almost unchanged in terms of its layout and urban scale for roughly a thousand years. Most buildings in the centre are at least 500 years old. Some go back much further.

The now ruined St Andrew's Cathedral, for example, was once the most important religious site in the whole of Europe, attracting pilgrims from all over the continent. Consecrated by Robert the Bruce around 1300, the cathedral and consequently the town flourished for the next 250 years. But at the height of the Reformation in the 1500s, the building was trashed by a Protestant mob following a rousing sermon by firebrand preacher, John Knox. The building was abandoned, and the stonework became a source of recycled construction material for the region. Still standing tall amongst the ruins is the 1000-year-old tower of St Rule's Church, a building that preceded the cathedral. The top affords stunning 360-degree views of the cathedral, cemetery, town, ocean, and harbour.

The three main roads: North, South, and Market Streets, are set on axis with the cathedral and tower which in medieval times would have guided pilgrims to their destination. North and South Streets are both lined with ancient university buildings looking like mini-Hogwarts with their towers and battlements. Between them lies Market Street, lined with small speciality shops, narrow at the ends but broadened in the middle to form a marketplace. The whole ensemble of roads and buildings speaks to me (nay, shouts at me) of a thriving medieval life of religious fervour, academic learning, and bustling activity. Furthermore, the patina of layered and patched stonework, visible evidence of recycling and reuse over many centuries, tells stories of successive periods of human progress followed inevitably by periods of decline. This is one of the things I love most about living in Europe – being at once reminded of the luminosity and achievement as well as the frailty and impermanence of our civilisation.

Journeys

Scotland's two best-known cities are, of course, Edinburgh and Glasgow; and what different places they are! I love them both but for quite different reasons. Edinburgh is, at its core, another medieval city. Glasgow is much more modern and mercantile. Edinburgh has, in fact, a split personality – the old and the new. The Old Town, centred on the Royal Mile and Castle, is famous for its urban density, steep narrow lanes, and street life. The Royal Mile forms a spine anchored at each end by two buildings that could not be more different. Edinburgh Castle (below left) is located at its head and the new architecturally flamboyant parliamentary building (below right) at its base.

Between them lies a mile of historical and cultural magic, particularly during August when the world's most famous festival of the arts completely takes over the town. I have been to four Edinburgh Festivals now, two in the '70s with my actor girlfriend, Helen, and two in recent times. I count them amongst the most memorable cultural experiences of my life.

# Journeys

Edinburgh's New Town is separated from the Old by a narrow but topographically dramatic strip of open green space. New Town is as distinctive as the Old but strongly contrasting, with its formal street layout, splendid Georgian architecture, and unified urban fabric. Set amongst it are some wonderful opportunities for adventure and escape. One of my favourites is Leith Walk, a river-side path that passes almost secretly through a densely vegetated ravine with a deep and fast-flowing river. It leads to the Scottish National Gallery of Modern Art, which is really two galleries in one, both distinctive in their own right for their neo-classical architecture, housing some quite radical contemporary art.

Edinburgh is a city bursting with art galleries. One of my favourites is the National Portrait Gallery, another distinctive historical building, recently refurbished in slick, minimalist style. The contrast between new and old could not be starker, but the intervention is all the more successful for that. And then there are Edinburgh's two most visited art museums (in good part because of their location in the middle of that nature strip between the Old and New Towns), the Royal Scottish Academy and Scottish National Gallery. And these are just the institutional galleries; there is a myriad of small private galleries as well. Edinburgh truly is a city for the art lover.

## Journeys

But the *House* for an Art Lover is in Glasgow, a city that to me, means just one thing – architect, Charles Rennie Mackintosh. CRM is one of my architectural heroes; I adore his work. He was designing around the beginning of the twentieth century. This was the period of Art Nouveau and Mackintosh was the foremost proponent of the style in Britain. He was very much aided by his wife, Margaret McDonald, the artistic talent behind much of his decorative work. But Mackintosh was not just a designer of eye candy. He was a foremost pioneer of modernism, one of the few architects of his generation to embrace and combine the decorative and symbolic elements of Art Nouveau with the restraint and functionality of modernism. In so doing, he melded two ostensibly incongruous styles. The two buildings which I most admire for this wizardry are the House for an Art Lover and the Glasgow School of Arts.

The House for an Art Lover was designed for a competition in 1901 but not built until 1996. The building is not as Mackintosh would have envisaged, given that it was built 100 years later than intended, and it is a tourist attraction with a shop and cafe. But it still well demonstrates his amazing capacity to synthesise beauty and functionalism. It is a modernist building in conception but exquisitely beautiful in its detailing and ornamentation – so beautiful, in fact, that I am moved to tears whenever I visit. The room shown below, left, gets me every time.

I wept recently for the School of Arts too, but for an entirely different reason; in the last five years it has been gutted by two devastating fires. Designed between 1896 and 1906, The GSA (shown above prior to the fires) is/was considered CRM's finest work, similarly exhibiting his talent for synthesising the decorative with the modern. Its library (above, top right) was revered amongst architects as one of the finest rooms of any era, anywhere in the world.

I want to complete this mini-tour of my favourite Scottish art and architecture with something different; else you might get the impression that all cultural establishments in Scotland are housed in 100+-year-old buildings. The Burrell Collection of art and artefacts is displayed in a superb contemporary building designed in the 1970s. In 2013, the building was A-listed by Historic Scotland in recognition of it being one of the country's best examples of '70s architecture. It is beautifully set within a Glaswegian park and thoroughly integrated into the surrounding landscape. Huge outer walls of continuous glazing fill the building with light and offer sweeping views across parkland and into surrounding woods. The small design team included a young Norwegian, Brit Andresson, who emigrated to Australia soon after the building was completed. There, she taught architecture for 40 years. Brit was one of my professors in the '80s. She was a real inspiration, responsible for cultivating (with others) a distinctive 'Queensland Style,' both through her own work and also her teaching. I can still remember the inspiring lecture she delivered on the Burrell building; I vowed to visit it one day, which eventually I did, some 30 years later.

Now, to some of my favourite coastal spots. It is hard to know where to start because I have so many faves along Scotland's 10,000 mile-long coastline. It is so long because it is so indented; the west coast, in particular, is crammed with long promontories separated by fjord-like sea lochs which, now that I have mentioned it, is where I shall start, then make my way around clockwise.

## Journeys

The Findhorn Foundation (FF) has two west coast outposts on the neighbouring islands of Iona and Erraid, which lie off the southwestern tip of the much larger Isle of Mull. I know them both well, having spent perhaps six separate weeks on Iona and four on Erraid, taking programmes, retreats, and holidays. Such opportunities are one of the perks of being a FF co-worker. Iona is owned by the National Trust (Scotland) and administered by the Iona Cathedral Trust, having been purchased from the Duke of Argyll in 1979. Numerous smallholdings are privately owned by individuals, families, and organisations, including a retreat house at the northern end of the island, Traigh Bhan, owned by the FF. Iona's residential population of about 150 form a very tightknit and quite religious community. The island is famous as one of the key sacred sites in Britain. It is where, in 563 AD, Christianity first arrived on mainland Britain, brought from Ireland by the exiled monk, St Columba, and 12 companions. The religious order they founded was one of the most influential in Europe. Iona became an internationally renowned centre of spirituality, learning, and art that has drawn pilgrims to the island since the 7th century. (The famous Book of Kells is said to have been made on Iona.)

Devotees nowadays follow a route similar to the *Sràid nam Marbh* ('Street of the Dead') taken by pilgrims of old, which terminates at a 13th-century abbey that stands on the site of Columba's original church. In the 10th century, the island was twice sacked by Vikings who massacred dozens of monks and established 300 years of Norse rule before it was eventually wrested back by Scottish overlords. So the island is steeped in historical and spiritual significance; to this day, the atmosphere there is thick with mystique. Certainly, the retreats I have taken at Traigh Bahn (below left), including one with my daughters, have been amongst the highlights of my time at Findhorn.

Anna, Lib, and me in the porch at Traigh Bhan in 2006

Neighbouring Erraid, however, is very different. It is privately owned by a wealthy Dutch family that peppercorn rents it to the Foundation in exchange for caretaking. It is devoid of buildings but for a cluster on its eastern shore, including an immaculate 200-year-old row house (above, right) made of granite hewn from an onsite quarry and built by the Stevenson engineering dynasty which was responsible for the majority of lighthouses along the Scottish coast. Robert Louis Stevenson, a famous son of the family, is said to have written the novel *Kidnapped*, whilst staying in one of the cottages. The Erraid community of six or eight, predominantly young members, live there almost self-sufficiently and host a rolling programme of workshops. My visits to the island have been memorable mostly for the walks across a wild landscape of heather-strewn peat bogs, massive granite outcrops, and a stunning beach at Balfour Bay, so named because the fictitious protagonist in *Kidnapped*, David Balfour, washed ashore there as the sole survivor of a shipwreck.

Speaking of which, I have been privileged to thrice go sailing off the west coast in a small (24 ft.) yacht, at the invitation of my friend, Michael, a most affable and laid-back skipper. On one occasion, however, we almost experienced a shipwreck of our own. The navigation equipment and the motor were both playing up (usually, it was just one or the other). One windy evening we realised too late that rocks were looming just when the motor went on the blink. Things got pretty stressful there for a while, but we survived to tell the tale. Generally, however, it is destressing to be on the water – to get away from busy work and community life and be as remote and close to the ocean, to nature, as one is on a yacht. The scenery out there is quite magnificent and the company always congenial.

We once sailed between the mainland and Eigg, an island with which I have a particular affinity. I have enjoyed two week-long singing workshops there with master choir leader Bill Henderson and a dozen or so participants. They have been relaxed, intimate and growthful workshops with plenty of time made available for exploring the sparsely populated island. On Wednesday evenings we joined forces with the island's resident community choir in their environmental and community centre, housed in what used to be the Laird's manor.

Almost all of the smaller west coast islands are owned by aristocratic (mostly English) absentee landlords who enjoy them for an annual grouse shoot and the rent they bring in. But not so, the island of Eigg, at least not anymore. The small resident community managed to buy out the owner in 1997, having raised £1.5m by crowd-funding. Since the buyout, they have built an autonomous renewable power grid and successfully managed all their own affairs. Their example has inspired several more such community buyouts in coastal and rural Scotland.

Moving around to the north coast and another favourite travel destination, Orkney, famous amongst other things for its Neolithic ruins. I have explored the 5000-year-old world heritage site, Skara Brae (below, left), several times now and always find it fascinating. Europe's most complete Neolithic village, Skara Brae, is older than Stonehenge. Its excellent state of preservation offers a detailed and intimate view into the domestic lives of Stone Age Orcadians. The nearby Ring of Brodgar (below, right), one of Britain's most famous stone circles is similarly intact. And not far away, a new dig at the Ness of Brodgar is slowly revealing a complex of temples that will likely rewrite early human history in Britain, putting Orkney at the very centre of Neolithic cultural development.

I will complete this section on Scotland by returning, full circle, to the coastline of the Moray Firth where Findhorn is located. I know it best, of course, having explored its treasures countless times. We are spoiled for choice when deciding where to go for a coastal walk, a Sunday drive, or a weekend away. The region is much more developed than the west or north coasts, with a rich cultural heritage based on fishing. Findhorn, itself, is a well-preserved traditional fishing village with a once-thriving natural harbour and lucrative 19$^{th}$-century salmon fishing industry. To the east are numerous towns and ports (Lossiemouth, Buckie, Cullen, Portsoy (below left), and Banff, to name but a few) with fortified harbours that, for centuries, protected haddock, cod, and herring fleets from the ravages of North Sea storms. And then there are my two favourite villages, Crovie (below right) and Pennan, comprising just a single row of houses perilously located on an exposed ledge at the bottom of a hillside. The former was famously flattened by a storm in 1953 and the latter, even more famously immortalised in the film, Local Hero (1983) starring Burt Lancaster.

All of these coastal towns to the east of Findhorn, plus a myriad of smaller villages in between them, are linked by the Moray Coastal Trail, which provides walking access to sandy beaches, steep cliffs, and dramatic rock formations including caves once used by smugglers. The connecting path is symbolic of the social, cultural, and economic ties that bind these communities. For hundreds of years, their common economy was based solely on fishing. Their shared religious traditions (Celtic-Christian fused with pagan) as well as languages and dialect (Gaelic and Scots), formed a distinctive and unifying culture. But, as fish stocks dramatically declined through the late 20$^{th}$ century, the industry collapsed to just a remnant.

Fortunately, tourism and whisky (and, unfortunately, North Sea oil and gas) have ascended to partly fill the void. Yet we still have one of the highest rates of unemployment in the UK. In recent decades, housing stocks have been eroded by the triple menace of Airbnb, gentrification, and second-home buying, such that the next generation can now find no place here. It is a tale of woe that is repeated all around the coast of Britain. Yet there are also grounds for optimism. Some communities, such as that on Eigg, provide inspiring examples of resilience and innovation. Indigenous languages and traditions are in revival. Throughout Scotland, there is cultural and political renewal and fervour around future independence. It is truly a fascinating country in which to live.

The Summer Isles on the west coast.

# Q & A

There are a few stories and reflections that I would still like to share before concluding this book. The best way to do this, I think, might be to respond to selected questions from StoryWorth that have landed in my email Inbox every Monday and, largely, gone unanswered. I hope that by the end of this chapter, I will feel that I am done.

**What do you consider your strengths and weaknesses?**

Mmmm, good question. One of my strengths, I think, is clarity of mind. Basically, I am a left-brain kind of a guy blessed with a decent serving of intelligence. I reason well and have generally applied my reasoning to useful purpose, not least in the realm of project management where I have steered some worthy projects in my various work and professional roles. And I have generally been able to deliver the goods, thanks to an equally generous serving of determination and focus. But of course, those very same attributes can also be a weakness. On occasions, and for periods, I have been fixated and inflexible in my thinking. My ability to focus has enabled me to achieve stuff, but it has also sometimes been a pain for those around me, especially family members. I have been guilty at times of neglecting their needs and wants or just been plain absent when I could have been more available and present. And in the workplace, I know that I have been difficult to work with at times, being so intensely driven and overly assertive when colleagues may have had a different viewpoint.

Another of my strengths, I believe, is my big heart, which may seem contradictory to what I just wrote. But it is a separate and equally strong aspect of my personality. However, it is true that my head has often overridden or blinded my heart; it seems that I am not well integrated in that way – somewhat of a split personality, perhaps. Anyway, I have always carried a great well of love in my heart, which these days, seeks to spill out with the slightest provocation. Being loving comes naturally with family, as it does for most people, I imagine. But I am blessed, too, with love for just about anyone and everyone else. The problem has been, and this is a weakness, that I am not always good at expressing it appropriately. And I have been told that I have a quite serious demeanour, which has given some folk the impression that I am crusty or even scary. So it has not always been easy to communicate and share the love that I carry. Fortunately, Findhorn has worked wonders for me in that regard, softening my shell and showing me how to express and also receive love. That has been a big part of my journey here.

Another aspect of my openheartedness is a propensity for weeping. I can shed tears with the least provocation, for example: when listening to soulful music, viewing a beautiful painting, reading a meaningful poem, or at the end of just about any touching movie that I watch. I have chronic emotionalism, I suspect, which I recently learned is a thing. It is also a stroke symptom, so has been even more acute since that event.

As a corollary to all of that, I am an inveterate romantic, which is lovely on one hand, but it can certainly get me into trouble. I can be pretty ungrounded when my heart is stirred, especially when engaging with women for whom I have a spark. Over the years I have often let my heart (some would say my hormones, or perhaps another feature of my physiology) override common sense and then lived to regret it. The fallout has sometimes been painful for partners, lovers, and acquaintances, which has been the cause of much regret and a lesson I have been slow to learn. I could not be more sorry about that. But having now reached 70, I can feel that at least my hormones have learned that lesson because they seem less easily stirred these days. And to be honest, that feels like a blessing.

## Q & A

I guess the third of my strengths would have to be my integrity. Notwithstanding what I just wrote about my heart dictating the terms on occasions, I believe I have done what I set out to do as a teenager, which was to live a meaningful life based on a set of well-reasoned values and principles. That does not mean I have led a virtuous life. Clearly, it has not been that. But it does mean that I have lived a well-intended life.

I strongly believe in natural justice. Perhaps I would have made a good court judge; although I am not sure I would want the responsibility that comes with that vocation. I have been happy to fight for progressive and justice-based causes as a layperson. And for that matter, I have been committed throughout my life to the making of a better world. I am gratified by that, and truly thankful for the upbringing, circumstances, faculties, alliances, and timing, that contributed to that aspiration.

**Do you have any regrets? What would you do differently?**

Not many and not much, are the short answers. I have mentioned certain regrets I carry, around my behaviour in the realm of love and relationships. There is one other that I carry in my heart, though. I have always regretted not visiting my father's body, immediately after his untimely death. I cannot remember what prevented me. I was an undergrad architecture student at the time, and recall being in the middle of something pressing. But I should have pulled out all the stops. I have carried a lack of closure around his death, ever since. Some years later, a close friend and colleague of mine, who was a father figure of sorts, also died suddenly. And on that occasion, I was able to visit him posthumously. His body appeared as an empty container; it was clearly not *him*, not his essence. This was an awakening experience which I would recommend to others. It raised questions in me about what it is to be human and the nature of death, itself. It brought closure around my friend's death and, unexpectedly, a degree of peace around my father's, too.

**What is your relationship advice? How do you define love?**

Given what I wrote above, you might think I am the last person to offer advice on relationships. But it is a subject that fascinates me and about which I have done a lot of thinking, as I have about the nature of love itself. In line with the commitment I made to myself as a teenager to fulfil my potential in love (along with creativity and service), I have always loved with enthusiasm. And over the last 20 years or so, have done so with an added sense of adventure, dabbling in tantra and polyamory. As a social scientist, I have brought a researcher's eye to the journey and have written about all these topics in another memoir titled *Deepening Love, Sex, and Intimacy* (2014).

I believe, and also observe, that most relationships begin without much consciousness and tend to drift rather than be steered. Way too often, intimate relationships founder or fail for want of any understanding about how to do them better – how to infuse them with greater purpose or intent. As a result, the potential for depth of experience, learning and growth is never fully tapped. This is tragic, I believe, because a purposeful or conscious relationship can be a wonderful opportunity to learn and grow – the definitive personal development workshop, perhaps.

Sexuality is important to us all. We are hard-wired for sexual desire so that our species may perpetuate. All life is driven to procreate; life begets life. Yet as humans, we have almost uniquely evolved to be able to dissociate sex and procreation. (I say *almost* uniquely because Bonobo monkeys and a few bird species use sex, not just for procreation, but for social purposes. They have no mating season, as such.) But, despite sexuality being the life force of our species and central to our emotional wellbeing as individuals, we struggle to talk about it, even privately, let alone publicly. I am not going to enter into a cultural analysis here, but I think it is clear, even without substantiation, that sexual thoughts, feelings, and behaviours, are repressed and sublimated in Western, Christian, middle-class society, and most elsewhere else as well. And most of us are frustrated, unfulfilled, or damaged as a result. The taboos around sexuality in our culture are such that it takes quite some courage to venture beyond, or challenge, the norms. I have done so modestly through conscious and non-monogamous relationships and also in striving to bring greater transparency to matters of love, sex, and intimacy.

As for defining love, it seems to me that we need as many words to describe love as the Inuit need to describe snow. The ancient Greeks classified six different types of love. I think there are many more types than that, and an infinite number of variations. The topic is too big to tackle here, but anyone interested in reading more of my take on these matters is welcome to email me for a pdf of my book, *Deepening Love, Sex, and Intimacy*, or to purchase it from Amazon.

**What political issues do you consider most important?**

Just one, really – *fairness*. As I have reiterated throughout this book, I am passionate about the fair and equal treatment of all beings, especially the weak, the deprived and the vulnerable – those who, for whatever reason, struggle to meet their basic needs or defend their inalienable rights. I have used 'beings' rather than 'people' here because I do not limit this aspiration to humans but include all species of flora and fauna as well as each tree, river, and mountain, and planet Earth herself. Now, I know this is a big ask, and that some would argue that it is in the natural order of things for the strong to devour the weak. I would agree, but only where the conditions are *truly* natural, as in a long-established stable ecosystem.

Human society is in no way natural, nor has it been since the beginning of so-called civilisation about 10,000 years ago when we saw the first domestication of plants and animals, leading to the demise of nomadic hunter-gathering and the first settlements. It was at that point that our uniquely evolved intelligence diverted the evolutionary arc of our species away from its integral place within the balanced eco-system that was the thriving, living planet. After domestication came the specialisation of tasks and division of labour, then the rise of hierarchy, political control, abuse of power, oppression of the weak by the strong, and so on. Ever since, we have been a dysfunctional species with a distorted worldview. Of course, we are never going back to how it was before, except perhaps in isolated indigenous groups and a few intentional communities, but this is where I think politics does come into it. If I ruled the world, the role of government at all levels would simply be to restore what I see as the natural order of things, i.e., that every individual and every species occupies its rightful place and fulfils its integral role in a viable, sustainable (eco)system. Given that our society has become so out of whack, redressing the situation can only be slow and incremental. But redress it we must, else things will continue to unravel, and we will decline as a species until we eventually wipe ourselves out.

Now I will respond to the question as I imagine it was intended, rather than with this abstract, meta-picture that I have just painted. I think that political dysfunction is well illustrated in Trumpian USA as well as totalitarian regimes like China, Russia, North Korea, Turkey, Belarus, and so on. At the other end of the scale, the most humane politics are modelled by New Zealand and the Scandinavians. (It can be no coincidence that the former regimes are led by despotic men, and the latter countries, mostly by empathetic women.) My take on just and good politics is best illustrated by the socio-economic regime of those latter countries, namely a high taxation-high welfare system whereby federal government redistributes a significant proportion of the wealth by providing *at least* the following: affordable universal healthcare, free education, sufficient social housing, and the elimination of poverty. To which I would add the aspirations of pluralism, liberalism, and fair treatment for all, including non-human entities. New Zealand and the Scandinavians do relatively well in the protection of nature. NZ, for example, has famously granted inalienable legal rights to particular rivers and mountains. Of course, these countries are not perfect. They still operate within a capitalist framework, which is inherently exploitative. But at least they legislate to ameliorate the worst excesses, which is the opposite of what happens in the US, which under Trump, has legislated to deliberately deepen inequality and ruthlessly exploit nature.

**If you could choose any talents to have, what would they be?**

Ah, that is an easy one. If I could have my life over again, I would choose to be a jazz musician – specifically, a saxophone player. I love all kinds of music from folk through rock, early music to classical and even opera. But jazz is my go-to musical genre, the one I listen to most. And my favourite sub-genre is the moderns: Miles, Coltrane, Brubeck, Hancock, Armstrong, Getz, Gillespie, Monk and more. Of those, I listen mostly to Miles Davis. If I could choose to have even a fraction of his talent, of course I would; who wouldn't?!

I could also enjoy being an artist, specifically a painter, and again, from the modern period. I guess I am drawn to modernism because it was so inventive and open-ended. To be at the cutting edge of a brand new form of creative expression must be extraordinary for those with the talent. But similarly, I love all art that has something to say: everything from Klimt and Van Gogh to Banksy and Leunig, and from the pieces in my own modest collection to those in fine art museums.

**Who inspires you? Who are your icons, and why?**

Well, I have just named a bunch of them – musicians and artists. Although clearly, it is the music and the art that inspires, not the individuals themselves. Miles Davis, for example, was a pretty reprehensible human being, yet no one would deny that he is a giant jazz icon. I would guess that a genius in any field is rarely going to be an ordinary, decent human being. He or she is much more likely to be maladjusted, narcissistic, preoccupied, solitary, and not particularly nice to be with.

## Q & A

I am hugely moved and inspired by classical music of composers from Baroque through to Minimalism, with Bach, Beethoven, Brahms, Tchaikovsky, Mozart, Chopin, Satie, Debussy, Elgar, Williams, and Glass being my favourites. Folk and rock musos that reach me include Dylan, Cohen, Van Morrison, Lennon, McCartney and so many more. I adore sultry female vocalists, including Billie Holiday, Amy Winehouse, Diana Krall, Sade and both Astrid and Bebel Gilberto (Bossa Nova being another favourite style). I have always loved theatre and dance but have not been able to attend a lot of performances since the '70s. My favourite dramatists would be Pinter, Stoppard, and Brook. From literature, I was gripped as a youngster by the existentialist novels of Hesse, Kafka, and Camus, and inspired by romantics, Wilde, Lawrence, and Durrell. More recently, I have been touched by poets, O'Donohue and Whyte, and devoured almost all of the fictional works of McEwen and Murakami.

Moving from cultural icons to those from other realms, I listed my spiritual guides and political influences way back in the chapter titled Values, so will not repeat that here. I have been particularly inspired over the years by activists who stood up against the odds for what they believed was right – civil rights leaders like Gandhi, Mandela, and King; counter-cultural figures like The Chicago Eight, Leary and Chomsky; and climate activists, Macy, McKibben, and Thunberg. Then there have been intellectuals such as Buckminster Fuller and Marshall McLuhan,

## Q & A

whose ideas have changed the world. My architectural heroes are too numerous to list, but stand-outs include creative geniuses, Wright, Gaudi, and Mackintosh; pioneering modernists such as Corbusier, Kahn, and Meier; and regionalists such as Aalto, van Eyck and Erskine. And so many more.

Having listed all of these giants in their fields, I would like to make the point that I also cherish, and am equally inspired by, grassroots musicians, writers, poets, artists, and activists. I am fortunate to have lived in communities (Nimbin and Findhorn) where participatory creative expression is valued and fostered. Even during the recent lockdown with its social distancing and restricted movement, Findhorn's resident creatives have been hard at it, performing in the streets as town criers, singing and dancing online, staging a mini-festival, creating a wonderful outdoor mosaic, etc. I find this hugely inspiring and consider it a key feature of community life. I believe that these folks are, in a way, as heroic and iconic as the 'superstars' listed above.

**Who has influenced you? What did you learn from them?**

I am interpreting this to mean folk whom I knew personally, not the icons I just mentioned. I guess the first of these might have been a friend I had at the age of 10 or so. I think his name was Gordon. He also attended St Heliers Bay Primary although he lived on Auckland's North Shore so had to commute daily through the CBD. On occasions I would go with him to the city after school where, gee, did we play up! Gordon was an influence for sure, but a negative one; he was a very naughty boy, as was I in his company. Not that I blame him; I have an innately naughty streak, too. So perhaps we goaded each other. Anyway, we got into shoplifting and other acts of rebelliousness – I am genuinely ashamed of some things we did as not so innocent 10 year olds.

Two high school teachers left an indelible mark on me – one was malevolent, the other, supportive. Mr Kidson, my French teacher in Grades 8 and 9, was a nasty, sadistic human being. He took delight in verbally and physically abusing the students, in a way that would see him locked up these days. He would throw wooden dusters at them or slap them in the back of the head if they stumbled over their reading or translation. Equally horrendous was the verbal belittling that he delighted in meting out. I have always thought that my inability to learn languages was due to that experience. And the opposite occurred when I reached Grade 12. Mr Lowe, my maths teacher, was a diminutive Chinese man with a twinkle in his eye and kind heart. He took a shine to me because I loved maths and was at or near the top of the class. Mr Lowe took me under his wing and encouraged me in the subject, offering after-school tutorials and loans from his private book collection. My love for the subject deepened as a result and I started to fly with it. In my matriculation exam I scored 98%, I think, enough to get me directly into second-year mathematics in my first year at Uni. Mr Lowe's support seeded a passion for maths that has greatly enriched my life and boosted my career. Kidson and Lowe are the only two teachers' names that I can still remember. It is interesting and sobering to realise just how much of an impact a teacher can have on the psyche of a young student.

On kibbutz, I was allocated a surrogate 'father' named Jerry who taught me to play Bridge. I am not sure that I would ever have had the opportunity or considered learning if it had not been for his encouragement. Bridge became a life-long passion, nay an addiction, that I shall write about below. And on the same kibbutz another friend, Mike, also became a mentor. We worked together in the *pardes* (citrus orchard) where I picked grapefruit, six days a week for nine months solid, which you might think would be enough to drive a person crazy, but in fact, I loved it and never got bored. I guess it was my first experience of 'love in action,' Findhorn style. Mike was a primary influence in that regard. He was charming, funny, and unflappable – an evolved human being, I would say. Whenever the going got tough, he would declare, "What the hell?!" with a laugh and a shrug, as if to say that all things come to pass and there is no point in worrying or whinging. He was brilliant at buoying our spirits. I never forgot that, or him. To this day, I sometimes parrot, "What the hell?!" whenever I need to remind myself of the transience of all things.

As a mature-age architecture undergrad (aged between 35 and 40), I befriended several staff members of the School who were my age or a little older. I would lunch with them most days at the university's Staff and Graduates Club. Two in particular became very close friends and each became a supervisor, one of my honours thesis, and the other my doctorate. Michael and Greg were authentic, thoughtful, politically left-leaning men. They were intellectual but never overbearingly so and modelled how to navigate the demands of academia as a sensitive new-age guys. If it had not been for their influence and encouragement, I doubt that I would have dared set foot in that world of inflated egos and one-upmanship. Thank you, guys.

**How did you choose your children's names?**

Ha, ha! We wanted to name our first child Anarchy (or perhaps Anarky) because we favoured the political inference and liked the sound of it. But either my mother or Jane's said she would not speak to us again if we so named her grandchild. So we shortened it to Anna. With Liberty, we did not name her for several months, contrary to the laws of the land which require new-borns to be registered within six weeks. We decided we would wait to see whether she could 'tell' us through her nature and emergent personality what she 'wanted' to be named. And sure enough, she exuded a freedom-loving streak from a very early age, which prompted the name. I cannot guarantee the

# Q & A

veracity of either of these two stories, but I have been telling them for a long time so they must be true.

**What unusual choices did you make in child-raising?**

There were many. Jane and I were hippies, so relatively free-thinking and unconstrained by convention. I guess our very first such choice would have been to have a natural homebirth. It seemed obvious, as did opting to have our kids sleep with us for as long as they wanted. We also chose not to have them vaccinated. Then there was the choice we made to let them roam freely from the time they could crawl, which was probably pushing common sense given that we lived in such a wild natural environment. And there was the choice we made to rip them out of that idyllic situation and transplant them into the city, which definitely took a leap of faith. Choosing to put them into a Montessori primary was easy, but the choice of high school was less straightforward. Jane wanted them to go to the private school that she had attended whilst I passionately favoured public education. I won that argument (one of the few I ever did against Jane) and so they went to a great State high school where they fell in with a lovely peer group of kids and generally thrived. After that, there were few critical choices we needed to make for them; in the main, we gave them space to make their own. We respected them for the intelligent and grounded kids that they were. And as far as I know, it served them well.

# Q & A

**At what time in your life have you been the happiest?**

I have just been writing about it. Those years as idealistic hippies, living on a commune – years of home births and early parenting in a house we built ourselves, growing our own food and living the dream – were, without doubt, the happiest and most fulfilling of my life. Jane and I were very much in love and our lives were blissful, wholesome, and filled with purpose. Before Anna was born, I was not at all confident that I could be a good father, as I was a bit bookish and serious. But once she was born, it came so naturally, I need not have worried. Parenthood filled me with a joy that I did not know was possible…and it still does!

**Have you done drugs? What is your attitude to them now?**

Yes, of course. As a student in Sydney, I did lots of dope, some LSD, and mushrooms. In Israel, hash was readily available, even on the kibbutz. And in London in the '70s, we had easy access to all of the above, plus cocaine and speed at the occasional party. Much more recently (in the last year), I tried ecstasy with a friend for the first time and loved it. So I am still open to such experiences, but I have not actively sought them out for decades. I have not tried Ayahuasca, but I hear great things about it from those who have and would give it a try. I think it is valuable to use drugs as a portal into a separate reality, which then helps one gain perspective on the world we deal with day to day – to not take it too seriously, to know that it is just one version of reality and that there are other, quite different, interpretations possible.

**What hobbies have you most enjoyed?**

As a young kid, I collected stamps and as a teenager I enjoyed photography, operating a darkroom for several years. But by far my favourite and most enduring hobby has been the game of Bridge, to which I have been deeply addicted for about 50 years. I first learned to play soon after landing on kibbutz and, believe it or not, I played six nights a week for six months. I was aged 21 and working full time, yet spending my evenings playing cards when most youngsters were out consorting. My kibbutz 'father' Jerry was a keen player and took it upon himself to teach me. We played as a partnership and, as I say, you could get a game any night of the week, either privately or in the kibbutz club which played once or twice a week in the communal dining room. It was very popular on the kibbutz and throughout Israel. By the time I left, I was playing competitively in an inter-kibbutz league and I loved it! That passion for the game has never left me or even subsided, and for the last 20 years or so it has been possible to play online at any time of the day or night. But playing with strangers is never as satisfying as having a regular partner with whom one refines and improves technique. Bridge is a game that can only be played with a partner. Keen Bridge players always cultivate one or more regular partnerships and prefer to play in competitions rather than socially at home. I have had several regular partners over the years. My most enduring partnership was with Craig, an open, affable guy and fellow hippie on the commune at Nimbin.

When I first arrived at Tuntable Falls, I had been playing Bridge for about five years, first on kibbutz and then in London. I felt I was just hitting my straps with the game and was as keen as ever. But, not surprisingly, none of my fellow hippies played or had even heard of the game. So I set about teaching a class in the hope that I could find at least three others who would enjoy the game enough to want to play socially. All of my pupils but one fell by the wayside. Craig and I continued on as a partnership, slowly refining and improving our game. He had not played previously, so his game was based on my teaching. Therefore we had a very tight understanding, which at times verged on the psychic. We played on Tuesday nights in the Lismore club, about an hour's drive from Nimbin. And we began to do very well, regularly winning sessions against folk who had played for decades. Some of those senior club members took a shine to us and invited us to join them in competitions against other clubs. From there we graduated to playing regional events, held over a weekend in towns and cities around northern NSW and southern Queensland. We were playing very solidly by this time and began to win prizes – sometimes cash but, more often, minor trophies such as crystal glasses and the like. From there we progressed to

## Q & A

playing at the Nationals in Canberra, which we did for several years, and the prestigious Gold Coast Congress.

Somewhere along the way, we befriended a guy who was a top professional who had played for Australia. Paul took us under his wing as a mentor and invited us to team with him at a couple of Gold Coast events, which was a huge honour. Craig and I developed a modest reputation at the top level of the game in Australia, becoming known as 'those hippie Bridge players.' Given that our rise in the game unfolded in less than five years, it was quite remarkable and remains, for me, highly memorable.

But not unreasonably, Jane was not always happy with me disappearing for a whole weekend. In retrospect, I was certainly taking liberties, not least because our kids were still young. But it did not stop there. Once we got to Brisbane I picked up with a new partner, Gary, who became another very close friend. He and I played mostly in clubs, in and around Brisbane, but occasionally, at regional competitions. Our finest moment came in the Queensland team trials when, after playing for three days, our fate came down to the final bid on the final hand. You could not have scripted a more dramatic finish. Gary had a choice of bids to make, one that would get us in the Queensland team to play the Interstate competition in Hobart (all expenses paid). The other would see us become the reserve pair that would only go if one of the three qualifiers could not. He opted for the latter, so we never represented our State, which is probably just as well because I would have been out of my league in Hobart and a potential embarrassment to the team.

**What have been your biggest wins and losses?**

When playing in the Gold Coast Congress with Craig, we once qualified for the final, which was a feat in itself as we were up against the best pairs in the land, many of them professional Bridge players. And then we went on to win one of the three sessions, against all the odds.

Wow, what timing! I just now took a break from writing to play a round of my current Bridge competition, online with a regular partner who lives in Luxembourg. We play one round of this event every fortnight over four or five months. And we have been doing pretty well, picking up a draw or small win in all but one of our matches. But tonight we blitzed it, scoring a maximum (20-nil) result, which will leave us placed second with about four rounds left to play. Right now, I am feeling quite exhilarated, having not felt very bright all day. The win has certainly got the dopamine coursing through my veins.

But my most satisfying competition win of all, did not come playing Bridge. Rather, it occurred when I entered the annual

## Q & A

Queensland Professional Photography Awards in just my second year as a pro photographer. I entered in the Commercial category, which included architecture, interiors, industrial, and product photography. (Landscape, Fashion, Weddings and Portraiture were all in separate categories.) In those days I carried a Canon D30, an entry-level digital camera, which was a pop gun compared with the expensive, high-res, medium-format cameras that most professionals used. But I managed against the odds and all expectations (most of all, my own) to win first place. I got to call myself Queensland Commercial Photographer of the Year for 12 months. Judging was based on four prints only (which worked in my favour as I did not have many more of the requisite quality). We got to sit behind the judges as they critiqued and rated each image. It was a real education and the main reason I entered, i.e., to get some expert feedback on my work. The image below left was one of my four entries, all of which had to have been taken in the last year. (I had just returned from a trip to Europe and the US.) Below right is the after-party at Ric's Café in Fortitude Valley where I lived. I met and bonded with a whole new bunch of colleagues that weekend, some of whom were peeved that the Commercial award had gone to an upstart with a pop gun of a camera. (The folk around me in the photo are mostly wedding photographers whom I learned that night make about $200K a year.) The following year, I took the runner-up prize, thus proving that the previous year's win was no fluke.

# Q & A

I do not recall suffering too many losses in my life, but one in particular sticks in my memory like glue. I lost £30 to a classic street hustle – the three-cup trick whereby you have to pick the cup with the ball underneath. It is such a con and I should have known better, but I was so convinced that I had the right answer. Now, £30 may not sound like a lot, but back in the day when I was earning just £25 per week in a factory job, it felt like a huge loss. Combined with the humiliation of being conned, it so shook me that I broke down when telling my partner about it afterwards.

**What are your favourite possessions and why?**

I have very limited possessions and even fewer favourites. I am a minimalist, not a materialist or an accumulator of *stuff*. Indeed, I have deliberately reduced my belongings over the last few years. In doing so, I have regularly asked which do I most value and why. My art would be at the top of the list. I cherish my modest collection hugely, gaining pleasure and solace from it many times a day. My hi-fi, computers (laptop and desktop) and a coffee table that I made in the workshop at QUT, are also guaranteed a place on the list. I once highly valued books, having shipped an extensive library from Australia to the UK, 15 years ago. But these days I have just a few. And I think that is it!

**What are some of the best shows you have ever been to?**

I enjoyed numerous memorable shows in Britain during the '70s. London had a vibrant arts scene, despite the recession (or perhaps it seemed so *because* of the recession). I was privileged in 1973 to see the original Rocky Horror Show at the Royal Court Theatre in Chelsea. Another claim to fame is having attended the inaugural performance of Dark Side of the Moon, at Earls Court Stadium in 1974. I also fell in love with opera during this period. However, my girlfriend Helen and I could never afford tickets to Covent Garden, so our modus operandi was to arrive in time to catch the first act on closed-circuit TV in the foyer, then sneak into the auditorium during the interval and watch the remaining two or three acts whilst standing in the shadows at the back of the stalls. So I guess I have seen the second and third acts of about 30 operas, but the first act of only 10 or so. Helen was studying drama at the time and so we attended a lot of theatre as well, much of it amateur or community-based. But the play that I will never forget was called, The Id, written and directed by Peter Brook and staged at the Roundhouse. It was a portrayal of an indigenous African tribe falling apart under the influence of colonialism. There was no dialogue, as such, just deteriorating interaction and increasingly degenerate behaviour.

That reminds me of one of my favourite movies, seen at the same time – an obscure French film titled Themroc (1973). Surrealistic and anarchic as only the French can do, it similarly contains no dialogue. It opens with text over a plain background stating "This film is not in French or any other language." The protagonists communicate in grunts, groans, screams, and wails. Check it out!

**When did you have the least money? How did you manage?**

That is easy to answer. I was most broke whilst living in London during the '70s. I had decided it was time to return home to Australia after three years away and needed to save the airfare, which was prohibitively expensive. A global recession had hit Britain hard. Whereas two years earlier I was able to earn £100 per week on building sites, the only job I could find was testing electronics on a production line earning £25 per week. And from that wage, after living expenses, I had to save for a ticket back to Australia, which took almost 12 months. It helped that the rent we paid was just £6 per week!

# Q & A

**What is one of the most beautiful places you have ever been?**

Mmmm, that is a tough one; there have been so many. I would rate Bali pretty highly, so long as you can escape the tourists. Its natural and cultural delights are dense, rich, inspiring, and infused with spirituality and tradition. I have never been to India, sadly. I would love to, but it seems unlikely to happen now. However, experiencing Bali has been the next best thing. Being predominantly Hindu, it possesses many of the same attributes. Kyoto and other parts of Japan are also extraordinary for their photogenic beauty. One of my favourite sites in Kyoto is the Fushimi Inari Shrine. Its walking meditation trail, shown below, extends for four or five kilometres through undulating forested terrain. Walking it was one of the most memorable architectural experiences of my life.

# Q & A

**Have you ever gotten into a scrape while camping?**

I recall one such scrape from the time I was tramping (hiking) in the NZ South Island with a Habonim group of 16 year-olds. Somewhere around Nelson, we camped for the night. We spent the evening around a campfire and because the night sky was brilliantly clear, went to sleep in the open. I woke in the morning to find the bottom half of my sleeping bag burned, blackened, and still smouldering. Lesson learned the hard way, namely, to douse campfires thoroughly before going to sleep!

**Did you have a job while you were in high school?**

My first job was the only one from which I have ever been fired – stacking shelves in a pharmacy after school. I was 13, I think. I did not like my employer and struggled to be subordinate enough for him. It was my first taste of being pushed around by a boss, which I think contributed to my lifelong loathing of exploitative employers. He resented that I was not willing to be subservient, so he fired me.

Another mind-numbing job I hated enough to quit before I was fired, was on a production line in a Fisher and Paykel factory. I was stationed at a press, the kind that punches holes in pieces of metal. On arrival at work, I would clock in and go to my station where, on my left would be a crate containing 2000 flat rectangles of steel, and on the other side, an empty crate. My task for the day was to punch two holes in each item and transfer it to the right-hand crate. I did this for about a week before noticing that it was driving me crazy. The health and safety considerations were non-existent; I do not recall that they even supplied ear defenders.

Finally in senior high school, I found unskilled work that I really enjoyed – as a casual labourer in Auckland's port, loading and unloading cargo ships. I did it with mates from school and the wharves happened to be in the centre of town, so we had a choice of pubs to go to for lunch. Being a 'seagull,' as it was called, was the most lucrative casual work available to a youngster, but it was very unpredictable. We would show up at six in the morning and wait to be called. Sometimes there was work for a day or half-day but other times, nothing. Before containers, which came in a few years later, the handling of cargo was very labour intensive. We would either be down in the ship's hold loading goods, box by box, onto pallets or up on the wharf, unloading and stacking. The work was hard, but exciting in its rhythm, tempo, and inherent dangers. And it felt like we were participating in the flow of life-force, in and out of the country. I loved it!

**What sports have you played? Which teams did you support?**

Dad was an accomplished sportsman. I was not, although I tried hard, in part because I admired and wanted to emulate him. I played a lot of team sport as a kid: soccer, rugby, league, cricket, basketball, and rowing. I competed in school athletics and swimming events. And I enjoyed snooker, table tennis, squash, surfing, and golf (the only one at which I was halfway decent). I am short-sighted and poorly coordinated, so it was never going to happen for me. But I did, and still do, deeply love sport. I am not exactly sure why; perhaps it is something to do with seeing humans fulfilling their potential.

As a Kiwi kid, I intensely followed the All Blacks. There were no live telecasts, or even delayed ones, in the '60s. So when the ABs were touring Britain or South Africa, I listened to matches at two in the morning, on a transistor radio, under the bed covers to avoid detection. There was seldom a match I missed, which is still the case, today. As a teenager, motor racing became another obsession; I regularly attended the annual NZ Grand Prix with my cousin, David. The other sport I have always obsessed over is America's Cup sailing, again because NZ had been highly competitive in that arena for a long time. In fact, I follow any Kiwi team that is competitive internationally. It seems that 'you can take the boy out of New Zealand, but you can't…etc.'

**Tell us about a great moment you had while playing sports.**

Well, there were not too many, but there was one that I will never forget – it was a fluke, but it gained me a lot of kudos. It must have been in my last year or two at primary school. We played soccer during the lunch break. I was always one of the last chosen when the two self-appointed captains went through that awful process of alternately picking their team members. Anyway, at one point I took a corner kick and somehow managed to score a direct goal. I lifted the ball over the heads of the players with enough spin on it to curl it in between the goalposts. I can still see its trajectory in my mind's eye; it was a thing of pure beauty.

**What inventions have had the biggest impact on your life?**

First and foremost, the arrival of the personal computer turned my life around. As mentioned, my dyslexia really held me back at school and also at university the first time. But by the time I returned to academic study at the age of 35 (in the mid-1980s) personal computers, in the form of Apple Macs and IBM PCs, were becoming widely available. I was able to use the university computers for a couple of years and then bought my first, a Commodore Amiga 500. I taught myself to touch type and used WordPerfect, the industry-standard word processor at the time. Suddenly, my dyslexia was nullified and my inhibitions around writing went away. I no longer had to laboriously rewrite essays by hand just because I had miswritten or misspelt a word here and there. I could freely throw down my thoughts and return later to edit out the typos without having to rework the whole piece. It was a revelation and I never turned back. I became a proficient writer and quickly grew to enjoy written expression.

The increased availability and affordability of power tools from the 1970s also had an impact. I recall building our house in Nimbin, or at least the first stage of it, with very few power tools. They were available at the time but not at a price I could afford. However, I believe that carpentry with hand tools is much more of a craft than when done with power tools and I certainly value having had the experience. But soon enough I grew to appreciate power tools for the speed, efficiency, and in some ways, precision, that they bring to building construction.

Finally, I would add one more innovation that I greatly value – Computer-Aided Design or CAD. When I was an architecture student, drafting was done by hand on a drawing board. I have never been confident with a pencil, which I think is another symptom of my dyslexia. So again, when 3D CAD came along in the latter years of my architectural studies, it liberated my design imagination and thinking in the same way that word processing had freed up my written expression.

**Who have been your closest friends and colleagues?**

Beginning in school, my mates at Selwyn College – the ones with whom I played snooker and cards and got paralytic on occasions, were my first non-blood-related 'family.' And a little later but overlapping, my Habonim *chevre* (comrades) were the second. At university, my radical flatmate and fellow agitator, Che, was a very close and trusted friend. (Funny thing: just yesterday I reconnected with him by email – the first contact in 50 years – and it seems that the heart connection we had then is still alive in both of us.) Then, the four travelling buddies, with whom I undertook the trip through Europe in '72, became life-long friends. On the kibbutz, there was my 'father,' Jerry and my close confidant, Mike. Johnny, with whom I shared a flat in London after leaving kibbutz, has been a close friend, ever since. After returning to Australia and moving to Nimbin, my Bridge playing and building buddy Craig and I were very bonded. At university and since, I enjoyed close collegial friendships with my lecturers and thesis supervisors, Mike and Greg, and also, my clients, John and Sue. In Findhorn, I have had more such heart-connections than I care to count; it is the very nature of community-based relationships. Finally, over the last 20 years or so, I have had several intimate relationships, some more enduring than others, with lovers who have remained very close friends and confidants.

**If you could thank anyone, who would it be and why?**

First and foremost, I would thank my parents for all their love and dedication to my upbringing; my ex-wife Jane for the love we shared and for putting up with me to the extent that she did; and my children for their devotion, and the love and inspiration that they engender within me. My siblings, too, have been a source of much love and affection for 60 or 70 years. Nonrelatives I would thank for being in my life are listed in the preceding paragraph.

**What, if anything, are your religious or spiritual beliefs?**

I am glad this has come up. I have been a little concerned that by declaring myself an atheist, some of my Findhorn friends might take it the wrong way. God is much invoked in this community. There is nothing more revered in our culture than *Eileen's guidance*, channelled by our co-founder during meditation and assiduously written down afterwards. Eileen Caddy published dozens of books of these messages, which she perceived as coming directly from God. Indeed, God Spoke to Me (1992), is the title of one such book. The word, God, or alternatively, I, Me, or My (references to God), appear repeatedly in almost each and every message. Now Eileen's was *not* the Judeo-Christian notion of God. Rather, it was as she put it, "the God within" or the "still small voice within" found in other mystical and esoteric traditions. I guess the resistance I have to using the 'G' word, even in this sense, stems from my early childhood religious 'education,' of which I wrote in the second chapter. But that is not to say that I do not have some such spiritual understanding or belief. I do!

Rather than attempt to communicate what, essentially, is not communicable, because it is so ineffable and I am not that good with words, I am going to insert another quote here. It is a rather long one (more like an extract, or a series of them, than a quote) but I absolutely think it is worth including. It comes from another Jewish voice, whose writing I read extensively as a philosophy student some 50 years ago.

Spinoza and the Rabbis (1907) by Samuel Hirszenberg (1865-1908)

Baruch de Spinoza was a Dutch philosopher who was considered one of the great 17th Century rationalists, along with Descartes, Kant, Hobbes, and others. Spinoza strongly rejected any notion of a transcendent God and argued that the Ten Commandments and, indeed, the Torah, that holiest of Jewish sacred texts, were neither literally given by God nor binding on the Jews. It should have been no surprise then, that on July 27, 1656, Spinoza was issued the harshest excommunication, ever pronounced by the

# Q & A

Rabbis of Amsterdam; it was never rescinded. We do not know precisely what "abominable heresies and monstrous deeds" were alleged of Spinoza, but we do have extensive detailed commentaries on his alternative framing of God. The following interpretation is said to have come from Albert Einstein, who revered Spinoza. According to his paraphrasing of Spinoza's, The Ethics (1677), God would say:

> Stop praying. I want you to go out into the world and enjoy your life. I want you to sing, have fun and enjoy everything I've made for you…Stop going into those dark, cold temples that you built yourself and saying they are my house. My house is in the mountains, in the woods, rivers, lakes, beaches. That's where I live and there I express my love for you…Stop praising me. What kind of egomaniac God do you think I am? I'm bored with being praised. I'm tired of being thanked. Feeling grateful? Prove it by taking care of yourself, your health, your relationships, the world. Express your joy! That's the way to praise me…Stop blaming me for your miserable life; I never told you there was anything wrong with you or that you were a sinner, or that your sexuality was a bad thing. Sex is a gift I have given you and with which you can express your love, your ecstasy, your joy. So don't blame me for everything that others made you believe…Stop reading alleged sacred scriptures that have nothing to do with me. If you can't read me in a sunrise, in a landscape, in the look of your friends, in your son's eyes—you will find me in no book!... Stop being so scared of me. I do not judge you or criticize you, nor get angry or bothered. I am pure love…Stop asking for forgiveness, there's nothing to forgive. If I made you, I filled you with passions, limitations, pleasures, feelings, needs, inconsistencies, and best of all, free will. Why would I

## Q & A

blame you if you respond to something I put in you? How could I punish you for being the way you are, if I'm the one who made you? Do you think I could create a place to burn all my children who behave badly for the rest of eternity? What kind of god would do that? Respect your peers, and don't give what you don't want for yourself. All I ask is that you pay attention in your life—alertness is your guide...[T]his life is not a test, not a step on the way, not a rehearsal, not a prelude to paradise. This life is the only thing here and now—and it is all you need...I have set you absolutely free, no prizes or punishments, no sins or virtues, no one keeps a record. You are absolutely free to create in your life. It's you who creates heaven or hell...Live as if there is nothing beyond this life, as if this is your only chance to enjoy, to love, to exist. Then you will have enjoyed the opportunity I gave you. And if there is an afterlife, rest assured that I won't ask if you behaved rightly or wrongly, I'll ask, 'Did you like it? Did you have fun? What did you enjoy the most? What did you learn?'... I want you to feel me when you kiss your beloved, when you tuck in your little girl, when you caress your dog, when you bathe in the sea...The only thing for sure is that you are here, that you are alive, that this world is full of wonders.

Isn't that fantastic?! (Although clearly, it is a contemporary take; Spinoza wrote in Latin, actually.) The quote appeared in my Facebook feed, this morning, in perfect timing, like so many others I have used in this book. The way in which this happens, is central to our spirituality in Findhorn. We call it *synchronicity*. Indeed, Peter Caddy's autobiography is titled, In Perfect Timing (1996). This is something that I certainly do believe in because I have had it happen to me far too often for it to be attributable to coincidence or happenstance. In that sense, I have had it 'proven' to me. The proof is not scientific (hence the quotation marks), so there is an element of faith involved; I am cool with that, despite my resolutely scientific worldview. The same applies to my belief in *oneness* or the *connectedness of all things* and the notion of *a loving universe*, which have similarly been 'proven' too me. These too, are fundamental elements of our spirituality, as is the notion of God inhabiting Nature. And of course there is that other framing of God that deserves a mention, summed up in the famous aphorism, "God is Love." This is my kind of God, for sure. It is Spinoza's God, and also Einstein's God. And it is also quintessentially Findhornian!

# Conclusion

Dear reader, if you have managed to get to this last chapter without skipping too much, then 'God bless you' (or whatever the equivalent Spinozarian invocation might be). I doubt that I would have read it at all, having long held serious reservations about memoirs. I have wondered why anyone would read one unless the author was exceptional in some way, or a paragon. But I am reminded of an occasion when I was driving with Liberty when she was about three. We passed someone we recognised, and I remarked, "She's a very special person," to which Lib responded, "But Dad, *everyone* is special!" Wise words from a young bairn. So yes, everyone has a story to tell. Be that as it may, I realise now that writing this book has mostly been for the benefit of the author. I love to write, so the pleasure in the creative expression, alone, has been reason enough. But it has also been helpful as a process of recollection and reflection,

## Conclusion

which has revealed a progression to my life story that I never really clocked before. The insight has brought a feeling of completion or closure and with it, peace, and stillness.

I have been obsessively driven my whole life to achieve and to succeed. Even after retirement a year and a half ago, I threw myself into volunteering in a typically manic way, which is, I suspect, what triggered my stroke. (At the time, I was hard at it, hosting a crew of Italian journalists over several days.) Whatever the deeper underlying psychology of that tendency (and I suspect it is my inner child seeking parental approval), I am grateful for having been forced by illness to stop, chill, and take stock. The stroke, the writing, and the lockdown have given me time and cause to reflect on all kinds of things, including the inevitability of ageing and death. I have had the opportunity to look back and evaluate my life. And out of that has come the realisation that, actually, I have made enough of a contribution to be able to enjoy a quieter, less busy life now without feeling antsy about it. And therein lies my newfound sense of peace and stillness. Writing this book has brought me a great deal of closure and the sense that a new, more relaxed phase is now beginning. A quote from Thich Nhat Hanh comes to mind:

> We have a tendency to think in terms of doing and not in terms of being. We think that when we are not doing anything, we are wasting our time. But that is not true. Our time is first of

## Conclusion

all for us to be. To be what? To be alive, to be peaceful, to be joyful, to be loving. And that is what the world needs most.

There is one further question from StoryWorth that seems like a good one on which to finish. Perhaps my response will suffice as a conclusion.

**How do you want to be remembered?**

I think this is an interesting question for all of us to ponder because how we are remembered is a measure of the impact we have had during our lifetime. If a person's life has had no impact, positive or negative, then will they be remembered *at all*? I suspect not, along the lines of that famous thought experiment, "If a tree falls in a forest and no one is around to hear it, does it make a sound?" to which consensus answer is, *no*.

My response to the question would simply be to summarise what is in this book, the pages of which already carry the answer. The stories are my version of events so, of course, I am happy to be remembered as represented by them. I have tried to tell those stories accurately and sought to verify their veracity where I have been unsure. No doubt, those who have known me will have their own version of events based on their experience of me and the circumstances of our involvement. For those who have not known me, however, or met me only fleetingly, or are not yet born, then let them read a copy of this book if they wish to know me better. I would have loved to read a memoir written by my

## Conclusion

grandfather, Harry Jolson or my great-grandmother, our family matriarch, Deborah Meltzer. An effective memoir can bridge across generations. I hope this one serves that purpose.

There are five things, in particular, for which I would like to be remembered: my fatherhood, contribution, principles, passion, and love. I will take them one at a time.

Firstly (because it is the most important) I wish to be remembered as a father (and now, a grandfather). My girls are, I believe, the main reason for my being on this Earth. They are my greatest legacy. And now that they each have two delightful children of their own, that contribution to the making of a better, kinder, more loving world is that much greater. Anna and Lib grew up to become thoughtful, empathetic, and caring human beings. The careers they chose embody compassion and justice for the underprivileged. They seek to bring love and light into the world and through being so loving, they inspire love in others. I could not be more proud of them.

Secondly, I would like to be remembered for my contribution in various roles and vocations as: builder, architect, educator, researcher, photographer, project manager, and event organiser. The Roman stoic, Seneca (5 BC to AD 65), who incidentally was Spinoza's favourite philosopher, wrote in his influential missive, On the Shortness of Life (AD 49):

# Conclusion

It is not that we have a short time to live, but that we waste a lot of it. When it is wasted in heedless luxury and spent on no good activity, we are forced at last by death's final constraint to realise that it has passed away before we knew it was passing. Life is long if you know how to use it.

By Seneca's measure, I think I can already claim to have lived a long life. I have never been interested in "heedless luxury," nor spent much time in "no good activity." I believe that I have used my talents and my time to good effect. Importantly, as an anti-capitalist, I have eschewed doing so for personal enrichment or to benefit private enterprise but, rather, chosen to be in service to public institutions, non-profits, my community, and society.

Thirdly, I would like to be remembered for having lived a well-intended life, based on a set of values and principles that I established as a youth: I have sought to fulfil my potential in creativity, service, and love; I have strived to relate to others with authenticity, transparency, and kindness; and I have fought for fairness, justice, and equality. I set the bar pretty high when I devised those aspirations as a teenager, so it has not always been easy to walk the path. I am human, after all, with all the frailties and weaknesses that that implies.

Fourthly, I would like to be remembered for having lived with passion. I decided as a kid that this gift of a life is a unique and precious one-off opportunity. And as such, we are obliged to live it wholeheartedly and to the fullest. I have not held back. And I

## Conclusion

have been most passionate about certain things: *fairness and justice*, as exemplified in my liberal worldview and progressive politics; *communal living*, for which I have strongly advocated and have also practiced for about half of my adult life; our *human potential,* which I have strived to realise in myself and others; and, oddly, I have been passionate about the game of *Bridge*.

Finally, I would like to be remembered as someone who loved full-heartedly. I know this is something I have not always done well, for moments or periods of time. These failings are amongst my biggest regrets. I have my community (and tantra) to thank for most of my learning and growth in this area. The spiritual fundamentals of the Findhorn community have supported me to both give and receive love more openly and appropriately. My desire, now, is to live out the rest of my days with loving kindness as my spiritual practice.

As I have said, often, I have long been an atheist and a humanist, so unlike many of my hippie friends in Nimbin and spiritual friends in Findhorn, I do not anticipate an afterlife, as such. Like Spinoza, I do not believe in any manner of immortality except in the way that we, and our deeds, are remembered. And like Spinoza, I do not believe in the God of organised religion, i.e., of theism (which is the meaning of atheism, I guess). Nor, therefore, do I believe in any God-given truth or set of truths by which we must live. The best I can do, therefore, is generate my own, or

## Conclusion

else live life as a rudderless ship. I do not find the absence of a single divine being troubling. I love the autonomy and agency it implies, which then requires personal responsibility as well as ethical and moral choices. And because I believe that life is devoid of preordained or inherent meaning, the narratives I create, provide the meaning in my life, and a moral compass. The stories I tell myself about how I should live, are not *about* meaning – they *are* the meaning! The plan I set myself as a teenager to fulfil my potential in creativity, service, and love, *became* the meaning in my life. The love I have for my children, allegiance I have to community, and service I have given, also added profound and enduring meaning. Looking back then, I think I can confidently claim to have lived a deeply meaningful life… and to have done so with joy!

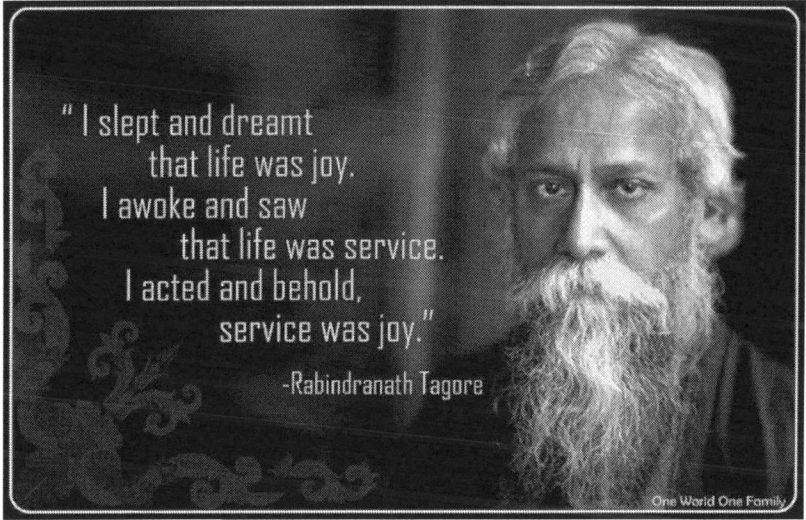

# Postscript

It has been six months since I began writing this book. And having now completed a draft, I am currently proofreading. Since starting, much has changed: there has been the lockdown; I have had a stroke; and, I have been on a journey of reflection and writing about what is important to me. All of this has greatly helped my thinking about the future. I have been reminded of the huge amount on offer here in Findhorn, thanks to the extensive physical, social and cultural infrastructure that has evolved over almost 60 years. But right now little of this is happening, at least not in person. Some of it has been adapted to online platforms: Taizé, Sacred Dance, and community meetings and meditations, for example. Yet, the Community Centre is closed, as are the Universal Hall and the Moray Art Centre. So there are few shared meals, casual conversations, parties, or cultural events.

# Postscript

Furthermore, we are heading into winter now (or "into the dark," as some describe it) during which we naturally become more housebound. This year, the sense of social alienation will be that much more acute. In the bleakest of all changes, the Findhorn Foundation has laid off 50% of its staff, many of whom are close friends of mine. Some will be moving away. The Foundation announced it is not planning to resume courses and workshops before 2022, which means that the Community Centre will probably remain closed and the activity and vibrancy that comes with the usual influx of guests will remain absent for at least another 18 months. So things are pretty grim!

On a Skype call two months ago, Liberty expressed an openness, indeed a desire, to have me come live with her and family in New Zealand. The decision did not take much thinking about; I accepted the invitation with alacrity and gratitude. I deeply love Liberty and her family, so living with, or close by, them is a delightful prospect. And it will be a real blessing to be just across the Tasman Sea from other much loved family members: my 90-year-old mum; daughter Anna and her family; and all my siblings except for John who lives in Dorset. And just last month, Liberty and Bradley managed to buy a house in the small coastal town they had set their hearts on.[*] I will join them as soon as I can. I

---

[*] Paekakariki, near Wellington, is of much the same size and with much the same alternative culture as Findhorn. I think I will feel at home there!

## Postscript

could not be happier about this latest unexpected turn of events, which effectively marks the beginning of yet another phase of my life. If I am lucky enough to spend the next 20 years living out my days in New Zealand, it will be as a matching bookend to my first 20 growing up there. How cool would that be?!

I would like to finish with a poem from a favourite writer, John O'Donohue – perhaps it is a portent of things to come.

### To Bless the Space Between Us
#### John O'Donohue

This is the time to be slow,
Lie low to the wall
Until the bitter weather passes.

Try, as best you can, not to let
The wire brush of doubt
Scrape from your heart
All sense of yourself
And your hesitant light.

If you remain generous,
Time will come good;
And you will find your feet
Again on fresh pastures of promise,
Where the air will be kind
And blushed with beginning.

OTHER BOOKS BY THE AUTHOR
(All are available from Amazon or from me as a pdf.
Email: graham.meltzer@gmail.com)

Another Kind of Space: Creating Ecological Dwellings and Environments (2003) (co-author, Alan Dearling)

Sustainable Community: Learning from the Cohousing Model (2005)

Deepening Love, Sex & Intimacy: A True Story (2014)

Findhorn Reflections: A Personal Take on Life inside the Famous Spiritual Community & Ecovillage (2015)

Printed in Great Britain
by Amazon

44403681R10165